LITTLE BOOK OF
THE TT

100 YEARS OF RACING

Written by Jon Stroud

LITTLE BOOK OF
THE TT

This edition first published in the UK in 2007
By Green Umbrella

© Green Umbrella Publishing 2007

www.greenumbrella.co.uk

Publishers Jules Gammond & Vanessa Gardner

Printed and bound in China

ISBN-13: 978-1-905828-24-1

Contents

Introduction – A Brief History of Man

ELLAN VANNIN, THE Isle of Man, stands proud as the jewel of the Irish Sea almost equidistant between the shores of England, Scotland, Ireland and Wales. Dissected by a central range of mountains with its rocky cliffs and long sand-covered beaches the island has born witness to countless years of change but has always adapted to survive.

The Isle can trace its history back to the introduction of farming in the fourth millennium BC and then the inhabitation of the Celts from 500BC.

During the Roman occupation of Britain the island remained largely undisturbed before taking on Christian ideals in the fifth century AD. From the end of the eighth century Viking occupation gripped the island and saw the formation of the Tynwald, the oldest continuous parliament in the world in 979AD. A century later in 1079, under the decree of Norwegian King Harald Hardrada, the island was pronounced the Norse Kingdom of Mann and the Isles with Godred 'White Hand' Crovan as sovereign. Turbulent years followed as the English, Scots and Vikings battled for control of Man. However, times change and empires fall and in 1266 the Isle was relinquished to the Scots by

Magnus VI of Norway under the terms of the Treaty of Perth which heralded a cessation of hostilities between the Nordic nations and Scotland.

Following centuries saw sovereignty pass frequently between Scotland and England until, in 1405, England finally gained the control it had been seeking. Henry IV granted Kingship of Mann to his loyal General, Sir John Stanley. Despite the family's Royalist sympathies during the English Civil War, the Stanley dynasty controlled Man until 1736.

By this time smuggling was rife on the island to a point that the Royal Treasury was losing upwards of £100,000 per annum, a fortune at that time. It was felt that something had to be done and in 1765 the British Government invoked the Re-Vestment act, purchasing the island in its entirety for £70,000 in the name of the Crown.

The modern Isle of Man with its population of 70,000 is a bustling place that capitalises upon its unique identity seamlessly blending traditional and modern. Tourism is now one of the

island's greatest forms of income and smuggling has been replaced by a burgeoning movie industry that in recent years has seen over seventy feature films and TV dramas produced since 1995 including Waking Ned, Revolver and Severance.

However, by far the Isle of Man's most famous export is its tradition of motorcycle racing that sees thousands of bike enthusiasts descend on the island each year for the annual TT Races. After all, they don't call it the Road Racing Capital of the World for nothing!

ABOVE Tynwald ceremony on Tynwald Hill, 1909

Laying Foundations – Gordon Bennett!

ALTHOUGH THE TRADITIONS of the greatest motorcycle race in the world are firmly entrenched in the soil of the Isle of Man its origins can be traced much further afield: across the Atlantic Ocean to New York City.

Born in 1841, James Gordon Bennett was the son of James Gordon Bennett Snr, a wealthy American publisher and founder of the New York Herald. Brought up in a world of opulence and extravagance the young Bennett served in the US Navy during the Civil War before taking over his father's business interests aged just 26 years. Keen to raise the profile of the Herald, Bennett funded the British explorer Henry Stanley's

successful expedition into central Africa to search for Dr David Livingstone.

As the toast of New York, it seemed as if Bennett could do no wrong. However, in 1877 excessive alcohol, a party at the May mansion, and an incident involving a piano resulted in embarrassment, social scandal and the calling off of his engagement to socialite Caroline May. Seeking a new life he left the United States behind him to settle in France, dividing his time between his 100-metre yacht, the Lysistrata, and an impressive villa at Beaulieu-sur-Mer on the Côte d'Azur.

Bennett continued to manage his publishing empire from afar adding to it in 1887 with the establishment of a new English language publication, the Paris Herald (now known as the International Herald Tribune). Taking well to the European way of life he soon developed a love and enthusiasm for a new and exciting invention announcing in 1899 an international race and the creation of the Gordon Bennett Challenge Cup for motor-cars.

The basic rules of the competition were simple. Contested over a minimum distance of 352 miles, each nation was permitted to enter a team of three cars each wholly constructed within the entrant's own country and weighing no more than one tonne. Drivers were to be members of the relevant national club. The inaugural Gordon Bennett race took place on 14 June 1900 between Paris and Lyon with teams entered from France, Belgium and Germany, however poor organisation resulted in many competitors getting lost en route. The following year, under the guidance of the ACF (Automobile Club de France), the competition was run in conjunction

with the already established Paris to Bordeaux race over a distance of 350 miles. A singular foreign entry took to the start line in 1901 – an English 50 horse power Napier driven by Australian entrepreneur Selwyn Frances Edge. Unfortunately for Edge his British-made tyres performed so poorly at speed that he was forced to fit French manufactured rubber in an attempt to finish, earning himself a disqualification in the process. Ironically, Edge had

ABOVE Charles Rolls in a Peugeot with a man walking in front with a red flag as the law of the time required, 1896

OPPOSITE James Gordon Bennett who established the Gordon Bennett Challenge Cup

previously worked as a manager at the London-based offices of Dunlop.

The troubles encountered by Edge were symptomatic of difficulties haunting the British motor industry at the turn of the twentieth century. For many years the Locomotive Amendment Act of 1865, known as the Red Flag Act, required all self-propelled vehicles to be preceded by a flag-carrying pedestrian with speeds limited to 4 mph on highways and 2 mph in towns and villages. Matters improved slightly in 1896 with the introduction of the Locomotives and Highways Act that allowed vehicles of less than three tonnes to travel on highways at up to 12 mph, increased to 20 mph in 1903 with the publication of the Motor-Car Act. These restrictions, coupled with a British Act of Parliament prohibiting all racing of automobiles on public roads had all but stifled the development of the fledgling industry as continental adversaries constructed powerful machines capable of 60 mph.

The 1902 Gordon Bennett Challenge Cup took place over a route from Paris to Innsbruck in conjunction with the popular Paris to

BELOW French auto manufacturer Marcel Renault drives in the Gordon Bennett Cup

Vienna Race. Of the 219 entries a mere six cars representing France and Britain contested the Trophy. The British contingent looked doomed to failure even before they had started as the twin Wolseleys of Arthur Callan and Claude Grahame-White arrived at the start five and a half hours late plagued with electrical and crankshaft problems. Edge, making a repeat attempt in a much improved Napier, only just made it to the start in time having been forced to make a last minute gearbox change. As the race progressed the lacking Wolseleys fell by the wayside joined by French drivers Girardot, suffering a split fuel tank, and Fournier with a broken clutch.

Only Edge's Napier and the Panhard of French competitor Rene De Knyff remained in contention for the Trophy as the race swept through the Swiss cities of Basel and Zürich and on to the Austrian border at Bregenz. Only one more obstacle stood in their way – the

1800-metre Arlberg Pass. Both drivers fought hard on the ascent but the Panhard had suffered a broken differential sleeve travelling through Switzerland and, although it reached the top of the pass, it could travel no further allowing Edge to push on to Innsbruck and victory. France had let the trophy slip away to the British!

Edge's unexpected victory posed a new problem, but one that would ultimately set the foundations in place for the Isle of Man TT Races.

ABOVE The Napier Team in the Gordon Bennett motor car race of 1903

Laying Foundations – The International Cup

THE REGULATIONS GOVERNING the Gordon Bennett Challenge Cup stipulated that the club of the winning nation would host the following year's competition and here lay the problem. With strictly enforced speed limits and an Act of Parliament preventing prohibiting races on public roads it looked unlikely that Britain would be in a position to fulfil its commitment. However, it was pointed out that the full title of the association was the Automobile Club of Great Britain and Ireland and so a plan was conceived.

Keen to promote tourism, the Irish parliament leapt into action and quickly passed the Light Locomotives (Ireland) Bill permitting the racing of motor vehicles on public roads. A course was chosen based around the market town of Athy in the south of County Kildare comprising of one 40-mile loop to be raced three times, and a second 52-mile loop to be completed four times. The enthusiastic Irish took to the idea with gusto and the 327-mile race grew into a two-week festival with many supporting events and races.

Four nations entered teams for the 1903 race – Great Britain, France, Germany and the USA. Despite showing well in the early laps Edge gradually fell back through the field suffering from problems with punctures and overheating tyres allowing the continental drivers to push ever forward, with victory ultimately being taken by Mercedes-driving Belgian ace Camille Jenatzy representing the German team.

The fledgling British motor industry at last realised that automobile racing was here to stay and that it was a perfect platform from which to promote their altogether more sedate machinery. As a nation, Britain still had a great deal of catching up to do – not only regarding technology but also in terms of facilities. What was required first and foremost was an exciting road-based racing circuit that would test man and motor in equal measure. Only with such a testing ground could Britain hope to compete on a level playing field with their continental rivals.

Julian Orde, Secretary of the Automobile Club of Great Britain and Ireland, was convinced he knew the answer and, in February of 1904, set off in his Wolseley touring car to meet with the Lieutenant Governor of the Isle of Man. Orde was greeted with unparalleled enthusiasm for his idea, with support echoed all the way from the general public to the Tynwald. Here was an opportunity for this small island in the

Irish Sea to put itself on the international map. Orde had departed for the island confident that his mission would be successful - perhaps in part due to the fact that the Lieutenant Governor was in fact His Excellency the Right Honourable George Fitzroy Henry Somerset, 3rd Baron Raglan who just happened to be Julian Orde's cousin. With Raglan's support a Bill was proposed to the Tynwald and passed with little amendment. Subsequently Royal

ABOVE Julian Orde, his wife and daughters, along with Frank Hedges Butler in 1908

Assent was duly granted by King Edward VII.

The first trials took place on 10 May 1904. To the delight of the excited islanders five Napiers, three Wolseleys and three Weir-Darracqs contested five 51⅛-mile laps of a course that started at Quarter Bridge in Douglas heading south through Ballasalla and Castletown before swinging north through Foxdale and Glen Helen to Ballaugh and onto Sandygate. The cars next travelled east to the streets of Ramsey before joining the New Mountain Road back to Douglas and Quarter Bridge.

Clifford Earp, piloting a Napier, recorded the fastest time, completing the course in just over seven hours and twenty-six minutes before finishing in second place behind Selwyn Edge in the following day's hill-climb from Lewaigue, near Ramsey, to Maughold Church. On the third day speed trials were conducted over a measured kilometre on Douglas Promenade. Once again Edge was victorious however, whilst returning after his fastest run, he lost control of his car and collided with the wall of Villa Marina sustaining serious injuries. Despite this the trials were deemed a success and Edge was selected alongside Wolseley drivers Sydney Girling and Charles Jarrott to represent the United Kingdom in the 1904 Gordon Bennett Challenge Cup.

That year also saw the introduction of a new race – the International Cup organised by the Motorcycle-Club de France. Held in Dourdan to the southwest of Paris on 25 September 1904, teams from Austria, Denmark, France, Germany and Great Britain took part although the riders in the British squad had undergone no formal selection. Victory went to a Frenchman, M Demster, whilst the British contingent finished well down the standings. The race did however provoke a barrage of complaints about the organisation and conditions facing the competitors, resulting in an agreement between the participating nations to form the Fédération Internationale des Clubs Motocyclistes (FICM), the forerunner of motorcycle racing's current governing body the Fédération Internationale de Motocyclisme (FIM).

For the 1905 International Cup the Auto-Cycle Club decided to run a selection trial in an attempt to improve the prospects of the British team. Once again the Isle of Man seemed to be an ideal proving ground and arrangements were made for the motorcycle trials to take place one day after the motor-cars had completed their events. It was intended that the motorcycles should compete over three laps of the same course as that used by their four-wheeled cousins however, with the roads carved up beyond recognition by the automobiles an alternative had to be found. A revised course was quickly formulated requiring riders to follow the original car route south from Quarter Bridge to Castletown and then north to St John's before heading east and back to Quarter Bridge – a distance of 25 miles.

Eighteen entries were received for the Isle of Man's inaugural motorcycle trial of which only eleven riders and machines arrived for weighing and scrutineering with several more failing to

BELOW A TT obstacle of water carts in the road on the Isle of Man

make the start line due to a mixture of technical infringements, breakdowns and crashes. Finally, at 3.30 am on 31 May 1905, WH Hodgkinson set out from Quarter Bridge on his first lap of the course and in doing so became the first person to ride a motorcycle in competition on the Isle of Man. Five more riders took to the start that morning, a sixth, FW Barnes, arrived late and although permitted to start could not turn over his Zenith and was forced to retire.

Charlie Collier, whose father had established the Matchless factory in 1899, set a storming early pace but, having crashed at Braddan Bridge, was forced to push his cycle back to Quarter Bridge to change a damaged front wheel allowing Ireland's Charles Franklin to take control. Franklin maintained his lead until halfway round the final lap when a con-rod on his 6 hp JAP broke. The charge for the finish was closely contested with victory ultimately being taken by J S Campbell aboard his Ariel-JAP in a time of 4hrs 9m 36s, a mere 30 seconds ahead of the second-placed Matchless of Charlie Collier's brother Harry. The Isle of Man had witnessed its first motorcycle race and motorcycle racing had been introduced to the Isle of Man. Who on that bright and sunny morning in May could have known that over a century later the bond would still exist?

For their efforts Campbell, Franklin and Harry Collier were chosen to represent Great Britain in the International Cup. Campbell's retirement of his Ariel after a single lap was followed quickly by that of Franklin on his JAP. Collier faired marginally better, surviving until

BELOW A 1905 20-horsepower Rolls Royce, the runner-up in the 1905 TT

the final lap before pulling into the pits.

International interest in the Gordon Bennett Challenge Cup automobile races was fading as 1906 approached and the withdrawal of the British and French teams sounded the death knell. In spite of this, the accompanying International Cup race continued as planned on a course near the Bohemian town of Patzau. (At that time Bohemia was part of the Austro-Hungarian Empire but is now within the borders of the Czech Republic. Patzau subsequently became known as Pacov). One might have expected that, with the demise of the four-wheeled competition, everything possible would have been done to secure the future of the two-wheeled event but it was not to be. The race ended in a sham as the Austrian Puch motorcycles of home riders Eduard Nikodem and Louis Obruba were declared victorious despite having been followed around the course by a team of mechanics who instigated roadside repairs whenever required in total contravention of the rules. Many a com-

ABOVE Darracq and Girling in the TT of 1906

plaint was made but none was upheld and with that the International Cup was abandoned for evermore.

Harry Collier, who had finished in a creditable third place without assistance, was inconsolable and it must have seemed as if the long voyage home would take forever. This journey would, however, herald a new chapter in the history of motorcycle racing. Accompanied on his travels by his brother Charlie, Freddie Straight, Secretary of the Auto-Cycle Club and the Marquis de Mouzilly St Mars, a suggestion was made that the British should create a race of their own and it seemed obvious to all that the place to hold it was the Isle of Man.

Early Years – The Marquis & the Messenger

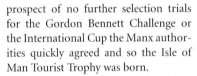

BELOW A 16/20 Sunbeam entrant in the 1907 TT

IT WAS NOT UNTIL THE JANUARY of 1907 that the notion of a new race became official. During the annual dinner of the Auto-Cycle Club the editor of The Motor Cycle, a popular magazine of the day, formally proposed a competition for motorcycles to be run on a similar basis to the existing automobile Tourist Trophy. With the prospect of no further selection trials for the Gordon Bennett Challenge or the International Cup the Manx authorities quickly agreed and so the Isle of Man Tourist Trophy was born.

Keen to capitalise on the ideas wrought during the journey back from Bohemia, Freddie Straight set to devising a set of competition regulations to preside over the racing of 'touring' motorcycles on British shores. His proposals were detailed and complex; included were measurements of bore

and stroke, specifications of silencers, sizes of tyre and the design of mudguards. However, when it came to their final implementation a far simpler criterion was specified: fuel consumption. It was decided that the Tourist Trophy would consist of two separate but concurrent competitions. The first would be for single-cylinder machines averaging 90 mpg, the second for twin-cylinders averaging 75 mpg.

With provisional regulations in place the next task was to devise a course. The original 51⅛ mile automobile route was considered too long and demanding and experiences of the revised 25-mile course used in the International Cup qualification trials offered little comfort. A route was needed that would thoroughly test man and machine but still allow competitors a fair chance of finishing; after all the intention was to encourage riders to compete and not to drive them away at the first opportunity! A solution was found in a new 15-mile 1,430-yard circuit starting at

Tynwald Hill in the little village of St John's towards the west of the island. Riders were to head east to Ballacraine before turning left and heading north over Ballig Bridge following the route of the current TT circuit on to Kirk Michael at which point another left turn was made to follow the coast road back to the town of Peel before heading back inland and back to St John's. With a field adjacent to the start providing ample space for competitors' entourages, race officials and interested spectators alike and its proximity to the draught beer of the Tynwald Inn, the route was considered ideal.

Having paid their entry fee of five guineas for works riders or three guineas for privateers, twenty-five riders readied themselves and their motorcycles for the start of the inaugural Isle of Man Tourist Trophy. Seventeen single-cylinder machines were entered with the tried and tested Matchlesses being considered favourites over creations from the Silver, NSU, Royal Cavendish and Triumph factories amongst others. The eight twin-cylinder machines included three Rexes, two

BELOW A 1907 entrant in the TT

ABOVE An 18 hp Darracq on the dip into Kirk Michael during the TT in 1907

Vindecs and a Norton all of which were considered state-of-the-art technology for the time. Practice was permitted to take place on the open roads but only before 8.00 am on threat of prosecution for any rider found flouting the law.

On 28 May 1907, viewed by an expectant crowd, Jack Marshall and Frank Hulbert sat astride their Triumph singles awaiting the starter's signal. At precisely 10.00 am two were set on their way for the first of ten laps of the St John's circuit. The tradition of starting riders in pairs has continued within the TT for the majority of its history. The pace was fast and frantic as the primitive motorcycles thundered their way around the narrow rutted lanes of the island. A truer race of attrition was hard to imagine as almost the entire field

encountered difficulties from broken suspension to punctured tyres, snapped drive belts to split fuel tanks. Oliver Godfrey's Rex twin-cylinder burst into flames at the mid-race fuel stop and was burnt to a cinder whilst another machine ignited at the appropriately named Devil's Elbow on the coast road causing Rembrandt 'Rem' Fowler to charge through the flaming wreckage aboard his Norton despite the frenzied signals from a flag waving boy-scout.

Rem Fowler's race was thoroughly packed with incidents. Exhausted by the relentless road conditions and having avoided stray livestock, suffered a puncture, crashed twice and stopped on a dozen occasions to change plug, he dismounted and was ready to retire until an enthusiastic observer called out that he was leading the second-placed rider by thirty minutes. Invigorated by the news Fowler leapt back on board his Norton and disappeared up the road in a cloud of dust and noise to take victory in the twin-cylinder category. Finishing almost thirty-two minutes ahead of WH 'Bill' Wells in a time of 4hrs 21m 52.8s Fowler had also achieved the fastest lap of the race averaging 42.91 mph, an incredible achievement consider-ing the poor roads and technical difficulties.

Victory in the single-cylinder race went to old hand Charlie Collier aboard his 431cc JAP-powered Matchless, his brother Harry having failed to finish the demanding course. Recording an astounding 94.5 miles per gallon Collier completed the 158⅙ mile course in 4hrs 8m 8.2s at an average speed of 38.23 mph having used pedal-power to assist in negotiating the many climbs. Of the twenty-five starters of the 1907 TT a creditable twelve survived to the finish, the last being FW Applebee aboard his single-cylinder Rex who arrived at the finish line some 1hr 38m adrift of Collier's winning time.

It is said "To the victor, the spoils" and this was certainly the case for the man from Plumstead as he was called forward by the Marquis de Mouzilly de St Mars to receive £25 in prize money and the magnificent winner's trophy. Donated by the Marquis, the silver trophy was based on the Montagu Trophy presented to the winner of the Tourist Trophy Car Races. Standing some three feet tall it depicts Mercury, the messenger of the gods, on a winged wheel and has been presented at every Isle of Man TT race since.

OPPOSITE
Scrutineering at the end of a TT race

Early Years – "This ain't no tea party!"

WITH THE TT MOVED TO September the Collier brothers returned in 1908 determined to keep their family name at the top of the leaderboard. Word was spreading about this new and exciting race and in response thirty-six

BELOW Gibson, Fowler and Harry Collier race through Umin Mills during the Junior TT

machines, fifteen singles and twenty-one multi-cylinders, were entered. With the first riders setting off at 10.17 am, the TT was once again punctuated by a series of crashes, punctures and mechanical failures. As expected Charlie Collier set the early pace in the single-cylinder competition but, despite being hindered only by a single plug change, there was nothing he could do to stop Triumph-riding Jack Marshall from taking control having recovered from a first-lap spill. Resplendent in corduroy trousers and a leather flying helmet, Marshall stormed around the St John's course to take victory over Collier by over two minutes at an average speed of 40.4 mph having taken the lap record in

the process. In third place was Captain Sir R K Arbuthnot RN who was permitted special leave from the Royal Navy to compete. In subsequent years Arbuthnot was promoted to the rank of Rear Admiral ultimately losing his ship, HMS Defence, and his life at the Battle of Jutland in the First World War.

The multi-cylinder competition was won by DOT Motorcycles-owner Harry Reed aboard a twin of his own design at an average speed of 38.5 mph. Second place was taken by J T Bashall riding a BAT ahead of R O Clarke's Belgian FN four-cylinder, the first of its kind to compete in the TT.

Another tradition established early in the history of the TT is that rules and regulations are there for changing and 1909 would be no different. Separate classes for single and multi-cylinder machines were done away with, a single prize being awarded instead. Furthermore it was decided that there would no longer be restrictions on fuel consumption but that limits would be introduced

on engine capacity, 500cc for singles and 750cc for the multi-cylinder machines. Silencers ceased to be a requirement but the fitment of mud-guards and saddles was still considered compulsory.

Having decided to experiment with larger capacity twin-cylinder machines it was once again the Collier family who was victorious. This time it was brother Harry who took the honours as Charlie, along with nineteen other riders, failed to even make half distance as reliability was sacrificed in favour of outright speed. And speed there was! Collier's winning time was 3hrs 13m 37s, an improvement of almost sixty-eight

minutes over his brother's winning time two years earlier, at an average speed of 49.01 mph. Riding a v-twin Indian motorcycle into second place, just four minutes in arrears, was American raider G 'Lee' Evans.

With Collier having set a fastest lap in excess of 52 mph at the 1909 race, the organisers, concerned by the high speeds now being attained, made fur-ther changes to the regulations for the 1910 TT by reducing maximum engine capacity to 670cc. However, the reduc-tion in engine capacity did little to reduce speeds as motorcycle manufac-turers continued to develop new tech-nologies at a phenomenal rate.

Interest in the Tourist Trophy continued to increase and, for the first time, Motor Cycle magazine set up wire transmissions providing 'live' updates on a lap by lap basis to fans in England, Scotland, Ireland and Wales. Back on the island an improvement was made to the course in the form of wooden-slatted banking against the stone wall of the Ballacraine corner. However, this alteration wasn't to everybody's liking, not least BAT rider Harry Bowen who, whilst leading the race, having set a new lap record of 53.15 mph, crashed into the boards ending his race and his TT hopes.

For yet another year the Collier brothers dominated proceedings, on this occasion achieving a Matchless one-two in fine style. Taking over from Bowen's early lead, Charlie stormed round the course to win in a time of 3hrs 7m 24s at an average speed of 50.63 mph, just over five minutes ahead of his brother Harry.

The TT of 1911 witnessed more change still. With organisation handed over in its entirety to the Auto-Cycle Union (ACU) the event started to take on an altogether more commercial nature. The Douglas Corporation set to constructing roadside grandstands in popular viewing positions much to the displeasure of the local community who considered that the race was as much theirs as anybody's. Furthermore the ACU, considering that the performance of the motorcycles had outgrown the course, announced that the TT would no longer utilise the traditional 15-mile St John's circuit but would move to a new, longer route that would become known as the Four Inch course – a name derived from the piston length specified

BELOW Harry Collier on the finishing straight, 1911

in the 1908 Motor Car TT run over the same route.

On examining the course the American rider Jack de Rosier exclaimed "Tell you what boys; I guess this ain't no tea party!" Never a truer word had been spoken about the TT. The 37½-mile course started above Quarter Bridge before heading along a rough track through Greeba and on to Ballacraine. Turning right riders would then join the familiar road to Kirk Michael used in the St John's circuit. However, on reaching Kirk Michael rid-

BELOW Tom Peek on a Peelers and W Creyton on an Ariel passing through Kirk Michael in 1913

ers would be instructed to head straight on towards Ballaugh and Ramsey instead of taking the usual sharp left-hander back towards Peel. Every scrap of power would then be crucial as the pot-holed road climbed for eight miles from Ramsey, past the Bungalow Hotel, to Brandywell and the highest point on the course. If the climb were enough to test engines and muscles then the descent into Douglas and back to Quarter Bridge would certainly test brakes and nerves.

Two TT races were announced, each to be held on a separate day. The first was a newly-titled Junior TT for single-cylinder machines of less than 300cc and multi-cylinders under 340cc, the second a Senior TT for 500cc machines of all derivatives.

The TT had come of age. Thirty-four competitors lined up for the start of the 150-mile four-lap Junior race on Friday 30 June, amongst them the familiar faces of the Collier brothers riding single-cylinder Matchlesses, Rem Fowler aboard a New Hudson and Percy Evans astride a Humber Twin Lightweight. Looking for yet another victory to add to his tally Charlie Collier fought hard from start to finish but could not match the pace of Evans' two-speed Humber which powered home to victory in 3hrs 37m 7s at an average speed of 41.45 mph, over nine minutes clear of the second-placed Matchless rider.

With thirty-eight machines entered the five-lap Senior race attracted huge interest, not least due to the inclusion of six bright red American v-twin motorcycles sent by the factory of the Indian Motorcycle Company with their litre engine capacity specially sleeved down to 580cc to comply with regulations. With the Collier brothers aboard their powerful Matchless twins alongside Bashall riding his BAT and Fowler on an Ariel, the British contingent could have been forgiven for thinking that the de Mouzilly St Mars Trophy was safe in their hands. The Indian team had other ideas and completely dominated proceedings before taking first, second and third places, albeit with British riders Oliver Godfrey, Charles Franklin and A J Moorehouse at the controls, the only American rider on the team, de Rosier, having fallen off eight times in practice and once in the race before retiring. Only Charlie Collier had managed to put up any resistance but, having initially been credited with second place, it

ABOVE Hairpin Corner

was revealed that he had stopped for an unscheduled and illegal fuel stop and was disqualified from the result.

As a side-show to the main event, a flying-kilometre speed trial took place on 4 July along the Douglas Promenade from Summerhill to the Palace. With a crowd of 10,000 watching it was left to American Jack de Rosier to take victory on his Indian. Covering the kilometre in 29.6 seconds at an average speed of 75.57 mph his Independence Day

ABOVE Competitors in discussion before the start of one of the races

had to contend with a vocal minority of Manx residents, lead by the novelist Hall Caine who lived at Greeba Castle, who were unhappy about the disruption caused by the TT Races.

Despite these worries, the 1912 TT went ahead as planned albeit with reduced entries. With engine capacity limits raised to 350cc, twenty-five machines lined up for the start of the Junior race as the sunshine and choking dust of previous years was replaced with heavy rain and slippery, mud-covered roads. The wet conditions had another effect on the race as machines equipped with belt-driven transmissions struggled for drive allowing those fitted with chains to take advantage. First place was taken by Harry Bashall aboard his chain-driven Douglas in a time of 3hrs 46m 59s with his team mate, Teddy Kickham, in second place.

The forty starters in the Senior TT enjoyed slightly better conditions than had been experienced in the Junior. Having led from start to finish, victory went to Frank Applebee aboard a Scott – the first TT victory for a two-stroke machine. In all probability the Scott team would have enjoyed a factory one-two had Frank Phillip not punctured on

efforts were perhaps consolation for his disastrous ride in the Senior TT.

For many, not least the manufacturers, the Four Inch course was considered too hard a test. Complaints had been registered about the condition of the roads and in particular the descent from Cronk-ny-Mona to Willaston Cross in Douglas. Furthermore concerns were expressed over the safety of the riders following Victor Surridge's crash in practice that ultimately resulted in his sad death. As if these fears were not enough to deal with, the organisers

the final lap losing almost half an hour in the process. Returning to form the Triumph team finished five machines within the top ten whilst the Collier brothers finished third and fourth on their Matchless twins with Harry taking the final podium place.

Come 1913 organisation of the race was becoming easier as organisers, timekeepers, marshals and riders all knew what to expect and where to expect it. Freddie Straight, having been instrumental in the creation of the TT and involved in its organisation, stepped aside with his position being filled by Major Tommy Loughborough who immediately implemented a new format to the Junior and Senior races with both classes being contested over two days in concurrent events albeit over different distances. This decision was met with much derision but did have the effect of encouraging new, smaller manufacturers to enter the TT. As a result 147 entries were received with sixteen manufacturers represented in the Junior and a colossal thirty-two makes entered for the Senior.

An unexpected predicament arose the night before the TT was due to start as Suffragettes campaigning for the right of women to vote littered the course with broken glass. With the riders asleep and blissfully unaware of the problems unfolding, a team of islanders set out with brushes in hand to sweep the course from start to finish under the guidance of Cyril Tomlinson Wynn Hughes-Games, the Vicar-General. Working through the night the last of the glass was cleared away at four in the morning leaving the course ready for the start just a few hours later. Exactly what the Suffragettes hoped to achieve

BELOW W H Bashall celebrates after winning the Junior 350cc on his Douglas in 1912

by their actions was beyond the comprehension of the Manx folk: the island having become the first place in the world to give women the right to vote.

Victory in the Junior was taken by

ABOVE Hugh Mason wins the 1913 Junior race

OPPOSITE Riders in the Senior race. In the group are McMeekin, and Rudge, (on the right), 1914

the two-stroke Scotts coming home in 5hrs 26m 18s, a scant five seconds clear of A R Abbott aboard his Rudge.

As the race continued to increase in size a new location was needed to accommodate the start of the 1914 TT. A site was found at the top of Bray Hill in the centre of Douglas much to the delight of the many riders who considered a downhill start to be of great advantage when coaxing a reluctant machine to fire into life. A new innovation was the introduction of metal letters attached to fishing nets hung over the road signalling distances to corners and potential hazards.

Overcoming appalling conditions, AJS pilot Eric Williams took victory in the Junior TT over team mate Cyril Williams (the two racers were not related) with a margin of 4m 44s. Their celebrations were, however, cut short as news of a horrendous accident was broken. Riding a Royal Enfield, Frank Walker had led the race until a crash

Lincolnshire's Hugh Mason on board a NUT (so named due to the factory being located in Newcastle upon Tyne) in a time of 5hrs 8m 34s at an average speed of 43.75 mph just 46 seconds ahead of the Douglas of W Newsome. Tim Wood scored another victory for

grounded him on the second lap. Undeterred he jumped back on board his machine and sped off in pursuit at such a pace that he crashed twice more. In a final effort he remounted once again and tore on to Douglas. Crossing the line after 4hrs 19m 55s he had amazingly salvaged third place but with an excited crowd now spilling onto the road he found himself unable to pull up in time. In a selfless act, he swerved hard into Laureston Road to avoid the spectators only to collide with a solid wooded barrier. Walker's bravery had cost him his life.

The Senior TT was an altogether more positive affair that saw Cyril Pullin claim victory on his Rudge with Indian's Oliver Godfrey and Howard Davis on board a Sunbeam tying for second place 6m 24s in arrears.

With the Isle of Man TT now established as an important event on the fledgling motorsport calendar its future looked secure but events in Europe were taking a dark turn and within two months of the conclusion of the 1914 races the continent was plunged into a bloody war. It would be a number of years before motorcycles would once again race on the roads of Ellan Vannin.

Racing's Golden Age

IT WAS WITH A FEELING OF excitement that preparations were made for the 1920 TT, the first to be held after the Great War. A decision was taken to modify the existing Four Inch course by removing the loop from Cronk-ny-Mona to Signpost Corner that had caused so much consternation in the past by heading onto the now classic Governor's Bridge. A further amendment to the course was required at Queens Pier Road in Ramsey although the circumstances surrounding this change were somewhat different.

When Julian Orde and his team had surveyed the island in 1904 as preparation for the Gordon Bennett automobile trials it was noted that a length of the Queens Pier Road lay in the private ownership of a Mr James Murray Cruikshank, the High Bailiff for Ramsey and Peel. Cruikshank was delighted to give his permission for the use of his private driveway and for many years the cars and cycles of the TT races went unhindered in their progress. However, Mr Cruikshank sadly passed away in August 1916 and after briefly being owned by a Scot, the property was acquired by Mr Hugo Teare. Teare's position was simple; for the use of his driveway he wanted a substantial cash payment. Not to be held to ransom the ACU and Manx authorities quickly devised an alternative that detoured from Parliament Square to Albert Road and Tower Road before rejoining the original route. Amusingly this late alternative would send the riders and spectating public past the entrance to Cronk Brae, Teare's home.

Communications around the route were improved by the installation of a special telephone system that allowed

split times to be monitored and incidents reported in super-fast time.

The 1920 Junior TT was won by Cyril Williams who had placed second in the last race run before the Great War. AJS team mate Eric Williams had actually set the fastest lap at an average of 51.36 mph but was unable to finish due to a mechanical failure, a fate which almost beset Cyril who, having

ABOVE Junior TT winner Eric Williams astride his AJS

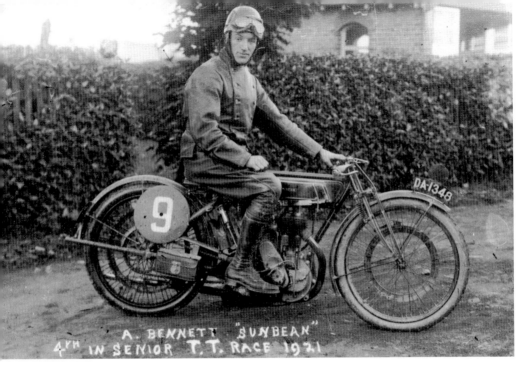

A. BENNETT "SUNBEAM" 4TH IN SENIOR T.T. RACE 1921

lost his transmission at the top of the Mountain was forced to coast and push with his feet all the way back to Douglas. Second and third places were taken by J A Watson-Bourne and J S Holroyd both riding OHV Blackburnes. The result of a new class contested within the Junior TT for lightweight machines of less than 250cc was dominated by machines from the Levi factory with R O Clarke taking first place in the Lightweight and fourth overall in the Junior.

Tommy de la Hay took victory in the Senior race at an average speed of 51.48 mph although the fastest lap was set by his Sunbeam team mate George Dance who, despite being a newcomer to TT racing, stormed round in 40 m 30s at an average of 55.62 mph before retiring with engine failure. Doug Brown's second place was greeted with much delight by the Manx community who were pleased at last to see a local boy competing with the best.

The organisation of the 1922 race was complemented by the arrival of a number of flagmen supplied by the Dunlop tyre company to assist the existing marshals. For the first time gold medals were to be awarded to the first three riders and the fastest team of three riders finishing within half an hour of the winners' time resulting in an increased number of works teams being entered.

Once again the AJS machines proved themselves star performers as Eric Williams leading a clean sweep of the first four places in the Junior TT accompanied in his task by Howard Davis (who was robbed of victory by a last lap puncture), Manx resident Tom Sheard and George Kelly. The Lightweight 250cc class was a far more varied affair with first place going to New Imperial rider Doug Prentice with Geoff Davidson second on his Levis and W G Harrison third on a Velocette.

Davis made up for his Junior TT misfortune by taking a remarkable victory in the Senior on the same 350cc AJS, the only time in history that a Junior machine has won the Senior race. In second place was Freddie Dixon, soon to be a familiar name in TT circles, with Indian team mate Hubert Le Vack in third.

The 1922 TT was greeted with the news that the Chief Constable of Liverpool had agreed to provide special treatment for motorcyclists travelling to the Isle of Man. TT mania was creeping to the mainland as even the garages located near the ferry started to offer parking facilities for solo and combination motorcycles.

BELOW Tom Sheard - first Manxman to win a TT

This additional interest was not going unnoticed in other quarters as offers were made to run the TT in other locations as far afield as Yorkshire and Belgium. Tempting as these offers may have been for the ACU there was a realisation that only the Isle of Man could offer the expe-

rience and quality of racing required.

Back on the island, the long-running dispute with Hugo Teare was at an end following undisclosed negotiations between him and the Ramsey Corporation. With the reinstatement of Queens Pier Road the TT had at last found its permanent course – a route that has lasted until this day.

For the first time the Lightweight TT was run as an event in its own right with riders heading out first on the road before the start of the Junior. Once again it was a victory for Levis with Geoff Davison at the controls. His time of 3hrs 46m 56s on his 250cc machine would have been good enough to take third place in the Junior. Although a non-finisher, there was another rider who had created a stir in the paddock: eighteen-year-old Walter 'Wal' Handley.

Despite having had his

application to become despatch rider rejected because the Army considered he would never be good enough, young Wal Handley had come to the attention of AJS rider Howard Davies. In turn, Davies decided to tip the wink to Ernie Humphries, owner of the OK factory, stating that Handley was good enough to win a TT and so it was that Handley got his first shot at stardom in that Lightweight race of 1922. His start to proceedings was not an auspicious one. Having readied himself for his first 5.00 am practice session he horrified onlookers and officials by firing up his bike and tearing off down the course – but in the wrong direction. It did not take long for everyone to realise that the young Brummie was something special as he lapped closer and closer to the lap record before unofficially breaking it by over three minutes.

Race day arrived and Handley was ready for the challenge. Powering away from the start to the cheers of the crowd he immediately broke the existing lap record on his first circuit from a standing start averaging 51 mph, an astonishing 5 mph faster that anybody had achieved the previous year. But to win you need to finish with fate on your

ABOVE Wal Handley tackles the TT course in the right direction!

side. Powering into Sulby at the most northern part of the course there was a pop, a puff of smoke and his race was over as an inlet valve on his OK broke. Handley may not have finished the race but all about him knew that here was a man who would undoubtedly take a TT victory very soon.

Tom Sheard became the first Manxman to win a TT when he took victory in the 1922 Junior in a time of 3hrs 26m 38s averaging 54.75 mph ahead of his AJS team mate George Grinton and Sheffield-Henderson rider

J Thomas. Fourth place was filled by a seventeen-year-old by the name of Stanley Woods who the previous year had attended as a spectator and vowed to become a TT racer.

Dubliner Woods had no experience, no money and no motorcycle but was

not the sort of man to let minor details like that get in his way. Desperate to ride he wrote to a number of manufacturers claiming that he already had a ride in the Junior TT and was looking for a machine to ride in the Senior. At the same time he wrote to some more manufacturers claiming that his ride in the Senior was already a done deal and that he was looking for a bike to compete in the Junior. Whether by luck, judgement or Irish charm he got a reply from the Gloucester-based Cotton factory putting a 350cc motorcycle at his disposal. Woods arrived on the Isle of Man expecting to find his shiny new Cotton ready and waiting but it was nowhere to be seen. Forced to practice on a friend's Norton he returned to his hotel and waited for news which eventually came in the form of two shifty-looking men who announced that his bike was waiting outside and it was broken! Working through the night he rebuilt the Cotton's engine and was ready for practice the next morning. In an interview some years later Woods explained that he knew he had to impress the two factory mechanics but had never before sat on an OHV machine and was unsure how to ride it. With his two factory minders looking on Woods flooded the carburettor, opened the throttle halfway and then the exhaust valve lifter and then on the official's signal pushed his bike down the hill. The instant he dropped the exhaust valve lifter the bike fired into life and tore off down the road

as if it were jet propelled as the little Irishman struggled to find the footpegs. The Cotton employees knew they had a racer on their hands!

Having observed the other competitors, Woods noted that a number of them had a small pocket sewn onto their leather waistcoats to hold their spare plugs so promptly found a local boot-maker to add one to his own. As he started his first TT race he rolled his machine forward as he had done in practice, dropped the valve to fire the motor and dropped all the spare plugs out of the undersized new pocket onto the road! Rolling backwards he bent down to pick up the errant items and secured them in his jacket before setting off down Bray Hill already 20 seconds in arrears. On negotiating Governor's Bridge on that first lap Woods felt that he had been taking the wrong line and decided to try something different the next time round. This he did to his peril as he ran wide at high speed and smacked both wheels into the high kerb just managing to stay on! The following lap he did the same thing but this time much harder and with a crack he sheered the exhaust clean off the cylinder. One might think that his race could

ABOVE Freddie Dixon won the inaugral Sidecar TT in 1923, but retired the banking sidecar in both the 1924 and 1925 races. Here we see passenger Water Denny cranking the outfit, right out of Governors Bridge

not have got any worse but it did. Whilst refuelling, Wood's helper, unaware of the old adage "less haste, more speed", flooded the fuel tank spilling petrol all over Stanley and his Cotton. With the engine still running it took but a moment for the whole lot to ignite in a ball of flame. Woods rolled around in the dust to extinguish himself whilst marshals doused his blazing machine. At this point most people would have called it a day and retired graciously but the plucky Dubliner was not 'most people'. Jumping back on board his smouldering machine he was refuelled once more and set on his way.

But the excitement was not yet over for the novice. Heading towards the left hander at Greeba Castle he applied the brakes but nothing happened. Somehow he managed to negotiate the corner far faster than he would have imagined possible. Woods brought his machine to a halt and made a quick inspection; his brake cam lever had split. Once again this would have been a more than reasonable motive to call it a day but no, Woods was here to ride a TT and ride a TT he would! Back on board he continued to hurtle round the island at break-neck speed for the final three laps, with only the soles of his boots to slow him down. After crashing several times he finally rolled across the finish line in Douglas to the cheers of the crowd after 3hrs 50m 33s to take an outstanding fifth place; not bad for a teenager from Dublin on a borrowed bike, and just a taste of things to come.

The Senior TT was dominated by a single rider: Alec Bennett. Aboard his side-valve Sunbeam he led the race from start to finish and in doing so set a record fastest lap at 59.99 mph and a new fastest overall time of 3hrs 53m 2s at an average of 38.31 mph over seven minutes ahead of second placed Walter Brandish's Triumph.

Just as 1922 signified the turning of a new page for motorcycle racing in the Isle of Man, so it signalled the demise of the Motor Car TT with only seventeen entries spread across a Junior and a Senior event.

BELOW Brandish Corner was the first circuit corner to be named after a motorcycle competitor when Walter Brandish crashed his Triumph there in 1923

Racing's Golden Age

EXCITEMENT CONTINUED AS THE 1923 TT got under way with the 250cc Lightweight. Aboard his OK-Supreme Wal Handley got off to a typically flying start and set a new lap record of 53.95 mph on the first lap. By the end of the next circuit he was clear of second-placed Jack Porter by three and a half minutes but Porter, riding a New Gerrard, fought back and took over the lead on lap three. Handley pressed on but, perhaps trying a little too hard, came to grief on the fourth lap crashing heavily on a loose-surfaced corner. With one handlebar snapped clean off, a missing footpeg and no fuel filler cap any normal rider would have taken off his helmet and sat by the side of the road for a cigarette but not Handley! Battered and bruised he leapt back on board and proceeded to ride two more laps, steering one-handed with a foot trailing whilst petrol splashed all over him and his motorcycle, to finish in fifth place behind race winner Jock Porter. For his efforts Wal Handley was awarded the Nisbet Shield: a trophy donated by former Chairman and Clark of the Course J R Nisbet for outstanding achievement.

The Junior TT was to prove just as eventful. AJS rider Jimmy Simpson set a blistering early pace, setting a record 59.59mph first lap to lead his team mate Charlie Hough by 23 seconds. By the start of the third lap, with Hough retired, his lead had increased to almost a minute and a half over a chasing Bert Le Vack of the New Imperial team.

BELOW A crash during the 1923 Lighweight race

However, Simpson's luck could not hold out and, in trying to avoid a dog which had strayed onto Bray Hill, he collided with Beardmore-Precision rider E R Jacobs. Neither rider was seriously hurt but Simpson's race was well and truly over. Bert Le Vack was now in control with Stanley Woods two minutes in arrears followed by a fast-closing George Dance aboard a Sunbeam who, to Woods' astonishment, passed him on the road and pulled away to a two-minute advantage and the lead as Le Vack was forced to retire with a lap and a half remaining. Woods was resigned to second place but Dance continued to push hard, unfortunately too hard for his Sunbeam which, having been ridden to the limit for almost 200 miles, gave up just short of Ramsey on the final lap gifting the win to the surprised Dubliner. Woods' win was a deserved one and the first of many.

RIGHT H F Harris being led in at the Junior race, 1923

Conditions were poor for the Senior TT as heavy rain fell and fog hung low over the Mountain road. Riding an Indian, Freddie Dixon took an early lead until valve problems caused him an unscheduled stop, allowing local man Tom Sheard to add to his 1922 victory in the Junior TT with his first and only Senior win.

Another new and exciting class made its first outing at the 1923 event: Sidecar racing. Fourteen outfits assembled for three laps of the full mountain circuit, the most interesting of which was that of Freddie Dixon. His Douglas combination made use of a special banking sidecar of his own design in which the passenger could use a large lever to either raise or lower the third wheel to improve cornering stability. Dixon commented that his unique design allowed him to corner up to 20 mph faster than a standard combination. With Walter Denny 'in the chair' Dixon set off on the course and a fast but steady pace unaware that the water-cooled Scott combination of Harry Langman and Ernie Mainwaring was closing fast. Then, just after passing through Ramsey on the second lap, Langman was on top of a surprised

Dixon. In retaliation he upped his pace to pull away over the Mountain but, desperately in need of fuel, Dixon was forced to dive into the pits in Douglas. Langman sped past but was quickly pursued by Freddie and Walter who started to close in as both machines hurtled down the road towards the sharp bend at Braddan Bridge. Then disaster struck for the Scott team. With the bit between his teeth it was obvious that Langman was carrying too much speed to make the corner so in desperation chairman Mainwaring hung out from the sidecar as far as he could stretch. Langman turned in but too hard and Mainwaring was bounced off the wall overturning the machine and its occupants. Unhindered, Dixon shot past and back into the lead. The excitement was not yet over for the Douglas pair as, with just over a mile to go, one of the mountings that secured the motorcycle to the sidecar broke away and the combination buckled in the middle. With Walter Denny pushing hard to keep the two apart, Dixon carefully negotiated the last few bends to take victory just 1m 38s clear of the second-placed Norton combination of Graham Walker and Tommy Mahon.

Yet another new class was added in 1924, the Ultra-Lightweight for machines of less than 175cc, which would, for the first time, be contested as a massed-start race. A mere seventeen entries lined up for the start on Bray Hill and after much close racing New Gerrard rider Jock Porter, winner of the previous year's Lightweight, took victory over F G Morgan riding a Cotton.

In the Lightweight class New Imperial rider Eddie Twemlow, competing in his first TT, took victory with a margin of over twelve minutes from the Cotton of H F Brockbank by coming home in a time of 4hrs 5m 3s with an average speed of 55.44 mph having already set a record fastest lap for the class at over 58 mph.

In the Junior an astounded crowd watched as Jimmy Simpson stormed round to break not only the Junior lap record but the Senior one as well, in

BELOW F W Dixon on his motorcycle with the broken sidecar

Freddie Dixon set the pace in the Senior on his Douglas and led for the first three laps, setting a new Senior lap record of 63.75 mph on his way. On the fourth lap he fell at Governor's Bridge but, with only minor damage to the bike, he remounted and continued to the pits to refuel. Forced to later stop for a plug change he saw the lead slip away as Norton ace Alec Bennett shot past. Dixon pressed on until Signpost, just short of Governor's Bridge, where again he was forced to stop as the front piston disintegrated and exploded through the exhaust. With the engine barely running he limped on to the finish line on a single cylinder to finish in third place behind Bennett and Langman.

In the Sidecar, victory was taken by Norton rider George Tucker after Dixon was forced to retire with yet more piston trouble on the last lap between Ballacraine and Sulby. In second place was Harry Reed's DOT over thirty minutes in arrears. Of the ten starters only five combinations made it to the finish.

1925 was a fantastic year for Wal Handley who was by now a seasoned TT

doing so setting the first ever 60 mph lap at 63.19 mph. Just behind were Wal Handley riding a Rex-Acme and Len Horton on a New Imperial, both of whom had also broken the 60 mph barrier. By the end of the second lap he led Handley by over three minutes having increased the lap record to 64.54 mph but at this pace something had to give and just a few miles later the engine of his AJS expired leaving the unlucky Simpson stranded by the road. Handley and Horton were also forced to retire as the race progressed so it was a surprised Ken Twemlow, brother of Eddie, who crossed the finish line in Douglas as victor.

veteran. Riding for Rex Acme, Wal's first race of the week was the Junior. Starting fast he sped his way through the field and at the end of the first lap was a single second behind Freddie Dixon who had himself broken the lap record. By the end of lap two he had grabbed the lead, an advantage he retained even after stopping for fuel. On the fourth lap he broke Dixon's record with a 65.85mph lap and proceeded to pull even further away from the rest of the field. With a final lap just a second slower than the record, he stormed to glory 3m 36s clear of second-placed Howard Davies riding an eponymously-named HRD. It was Davies who, just a few short years earlier, had tipped Handley for greatness.

Wal's success continued in the Ultra-Lightweight which, after a year as a mass-start affair, had reverted to the standard TT time trial format. Handley set off with a record-breaking first lap before grounding his exhaust and crashing at Creg ny Baa. After dusting himself down he set off again on a misfiring bike but held on through sheer determination to become the first rider in TT history to win two races in a week. Could the plucky Brummie make it three?

Starting in the Lightweight in his usual fashion, Handley immediately set yet another lap record, the first ever for a Lightweight in excess of 60 mph, with Jock Porter just thirty-four seconds behind. Handley maintained the pace and as Porter retired, his New Porter having broken a rocker, it seemed as if the treble was a certainty. But little is certain in the TT and on the third lap his front tyre burst on the approach to Governor's Bridge causing him to crash. With a badly damaged clutch there was nothing more that Handley could do so he coasted back to the Grandstand, his leather helmet hanging from the bars.

BELOW Alec Bennett in action

With Handley and Porter sidelined nothing could stop Eddie Twemlow from taking his second win in the class and a welcome victory for the New Imperial factory.

Jimmy Simpson set the early pace in the Senior TT, setting a new absolute lap record of 68.97 mph in the process. But his 498cc works AJS could not maintain the pace and within another lap he was forced to retire leaving the way open for Howard Davies to bring the HRD home to victory.

From the start the eighteen entries in the Sidecar were led by the Douglas combinations of Freddie Dixon, Fred Hatton and Len Parker but on the third lap things started to go wrong as first Dixon's machine and then that of Hatton fell by the wayside. Fortunately for the Douglas Factory Len Parker held on to take victory from the Nortons of Grinton and Taylor.

With the ACU under pressure from manufacturers who considered the spectacle of sidecar racing to be detrimental to sales, it was decided that the 1925 Sidecar TT would be the last. Race-goers and riders would have to wait another twenty-nine years to witness the spectacle once again. The future of the Ultra-Lightweight was also curtailed following that year's event. The ACU had specified that the 175cc machines should have a maximum weight of 150lbs (68kgs), a figure which the manufacturers considered impossible or at least dangerous

BELOW The line up at the start of the 1926 race

to achieve. Once again the factories would have their way as the class was relegated to the history books.

Despite a condensed programme with only three classes listed, the 1926 TT lost none of its thrill. Speeds continued to increase with new records being set in all the races and the island took on a distinctly continental feel with the arrival of the Moto Guzzi, Garelli and Bianchi teams. The Italians may have been on the Isle of Man in force but it was the Irish who ruled the Mountain course that year. First Alec Bennett beat TT greats Jimmy Simpson, Wal Handley and Freddie Dixon to win the Junior on his Velocette at an average speed of 66.70 mph. Next was the Lightweight and a clean sweep for the Cotton team with Paddy Johnson taking victory from team mates Morgan and Colgan, however, this result was not as clear cut as it seemed. Initially Italian rider Pietro Ghersi was credited with second place having finished just behind Johnson but an inspection revealed that his Moto Guzzi had been fitted with a different make of spark plug than that specified on his entry form. Despite protestations from rider and team, Ghersi was disqualified and struck from the result.

An Irish treble was achieved with

ABOVE Wal Handley has a tricky moment in the Lightweight race in the Isle of Man, does he fall off or doesn't he?

Stanley Woods' win in the Senior aboard a 490cc 3-speed Norton that was specially fitted with pannier fuel tanks to cope with an extended race distance of seven laps. It was, however, Jimmy Simpson who had set the early pace, first breaking the lap record from a standing start and then going one better by breaking the 70 mph barrier for the first time with a 70.43 mph lap. The crowd on the Grandstand were ecstatic! But ecstasy turned to dismay when on the third lap his engine expired and it was left for Woods to take his second TT title.

The 1927 TT met with tragedy before it had even started when Archie Birkin collided with a fish lorry on the course at Rhencullen and was instantly killed. Although the Manx roads were always closed for racing, no such provision had been made during all practice sessions; not that this ever tempered the speed of competitors preparing for race day. As a result of Birkin's death, a long overdue decision was taken to close the roads during the early morning practice sessions at future TTs.

Wal Handley took his trademark early lead in the Junior race, breaking the lap record on his second circuit at 69.18 mph, but crashed heavily at

Quarter Bridge on his third circuit of the island. In typical fashion he dusted himself down and jumped back on the bike to get on with the business of racing. Handley maintained his lead until halfway round the final lap when one of his pistons on his Rex-Acme overheated and melted allowing Freddie Dixon to zip past and on to victory.

Back on the start line for the Lightweight, Handley proved that he would not let this misfortune upset his game. Blasting away on the starter's signal he tore down Bray Hill on his way to yet another lap record hotly pursued by Alec Bennett aboard the OK-Supreme. Bennett continued to maintain the pressure, even managing to break the lap record himself, until, on the fifth lap, his oil pump failed. For once Handley knew his lead was safe and that finishing in one piece was paramount. Easing off he toured back to the cheering crowd in Douglas to take a popular win.

Stanley Woods, now a full time Norton employee, set off in the TT at blistering pace, recording 70.50 mph for his first lap and 70.99 for his second with Freddie Dixon and Jimmy Simpson in pursuit. Woods' Norton team mate Bennett, meanwhile, was

having to work his way through the field having started poorly. But Simpson's AJS could not take the pace and on the fourth lap he slowed and retired. By this time Bennett had caught and passed Dixon; only Woods was ahead but the gap, now in excess of three minutes seemed insurmountable. In all likelihood Woods would have gone on to take

BELOW Freddie Dixon being chaired by enthusiastic supporters after his win in 1927

another Senior title had poor communications in the pits not given him the impression that his rivals were close behind. Battling to the end, the clutch on Woods' Norton finally gave up over the Mountain on the fifth lap allowing Bennett to reverse his Lightweight misfortune to take a worthy victory in the Senior.

Alec Bennett's good luck stayed with him through to the start of the 1928 Junior TT. Riding an innovative Velocette KSS fitted with the world's first positive-stop foot gear change nobody could get close to the man from Belfast who proceeded to break the Junior lap record on three consecutive laps, his fastest at 70.28 mph just a fraction short of Woods' absolute lap record on a Senior machine, before taking victory by over five minutes from team mate Willis.

Two new names were welcomed to the roll call of TT winners as first Frank Longman, riding a JAP-engined OK-Supreme, took victory in the Junior TT and then Charlie Dodson finished first in the Senior aboard his Sunbeam as Bennett, Dixon and Simpson were non-finishers in poor conditions.

Dodson repeated his 1928 success a

year later in the 1929 Senior but, with a new absolute lap record of 73.55 mph, an average race speed of 72.05 mph and Alec Bennett almost five minutes in arrear, this time there were no doubts as to what might have been. The Velocette once again proved its worth as Freddie Hicks took the notable scalps of Handley and team mate Bennett in a Junior race which also witnessed the return of Pietro Ghersi who unfortunately was forced to retire with, somewhat ironically considering the 1926 debacle, plug troubles.

ABOVE Pietro Ghersi, astride his Moto Guzzi before the race

OPPOSITE Freddie Hicks being kissed by a fan after his win

No Limits!

WAL HANDLEY'S 1930 TT DID NOT start in the best of fashions as an unauthorised practice session came to the attention of the authorities. Fined twenty shillings for lack of a silencer and another five shillings for the absence of a horn, Handley commented on the irony of falling foul of the law for making too much noise and for making not enough at the same time.

South African visitor Joe Sarkis riding an OK-Supreme was a fast starter in the Lightweight leading Handley's Rex by half a minute at the end of the first lap. This margin was soon reduced to a mere six seconds as the Birmingham lad put in a new lap record but Wal's luck did not hold out and within another lap his machine was coughing and spluttering as his oil tank failed. Sarkis' machine soon went the same way leaving AJS rider Jimmy Guthrie to take the first of many career wins.

CENTRE A policeman watches Wal Handley push his bike off the grid

Rudge-Whitworth rider Ernie Nott set a new lap record in the Junior TT before being pipped to the post by his team mate Henry Tyrell-Smith with another Rudge rider, Graham Walker, taking third spot. Walker had been accompanied to the island by his five-year-old son, a young lad by the name of Murray who was already taking a keen interest in motor sport.

Wal Handley had been due to ride a Belgian FN machine in the Senior but the factory had been unable to prepare his bike on time. Rather than have a TT without one of its heroes, the ACU assisted in making new arrangements and a ride was found with the successful Rudge works team. As if to prove a

manufacturer that would last the best part of the decade. That manufacturer was Norton.

The early laps of the Junior were dominated by the Nortons of Woods and Simpson with Ernie Nott, riding for the Rudge factory, hot in pursuit. But it was the fast moving Norton of Tim Hunt, having recovered from plug difficulties on the first lap, which proceeded to set the pace. As Woods contended with a faulty steering damper and Simpson slowed with engine problems, Hunt charged onwards to a new class lap record and victory – a feat he repeated in the Senior event in which, on roads damp from the morning rain,

point Handley quickly got into the swing of things and set a new record of over 76 mph on his opening lap breaking it again on the third lap at 76.28 mph. As the race progressed, conditions worsened, the rain started and a fog descended over the Mountain but Wal just kept going flat out to lead the race from start to finish ahead of Walker and Jimmy Simpson. Handley's all out ride had bagged him the fastest ever lap, the fastest overall race speed and the honour of being the first rider to lap in less than 30 minutes. He also had become the first rider in history to have won the TT in four separate classes.

The TT of 1931 signalled the start of a period of domination for one

BELOW A TT motorcycle being refuelled on the quayside, 1930

he became the first rider to lap the island in excess of 80 mph. Riding the big Norton to its utter limit, Hunt had swept into the pits to refuel only to have the engine cut out three yards short of the box with not a single drop of petrol left in the tank.

The Lightweight did, however, give another manufacturer a welcome look in: the Rudge-Whitworth factory of Coventry. Ernie Nott set the early pace aboard his radial valved 250cc machine with team mates Henry Tyrell-Smith and the not-so-lightweight Graham Walker; he did weigh fourteen and a half stone after all, in second and third places. On the next two laps Nott broke the lap record twice taking the Lightweights past the 70 mph barrier for the first time ever but then, on the final lap, disaster struck as rider and machine parted company on the Ramsey side of the mountain. Walker, determined to close the two minute gap, was already on a charge as Nott remounted and headed towards the finish. Again Nott's luck deserted him, this time at Governor's Bridge, as once more he fell from his ailing machine. Walker's tenacity had paid off. Crossing the

BELOW The start of a race in 1930

finish line the popular Scot had done enough to secure his first TT victory ahead of team mate Tyrell-Smith whilst Nott, to the cheers of the crowd, secured fourth behind the New Imperial of Ted Mellors.

Still riding for Rudge, Walker once again found himself teamed up with Tyrell-Smith and Nott for the 1932 TT but there was also a new member of the squad in the form of Wal Handley who had abandoned hopes of any success on the Belgian FN machines. A trademark start saw Handley take his ubiquitous lap record on the first lap pursued by Nott but, on the fifth lap, problems with plugs caused both competitors' pace to drop sufficiently for New Imperial rider Leo Davenport to take over the running. Nott fought back and managed to take back the lead only to lose it when once again the questionable reliability of the plugs caused further problems allowing Davenport to ride home for his first TT victory.

By comparison the Junior was a simple affair to follow. Norton rider Stanley Woods was unstoppable! Tearing down Bray Hill and round Quarter Bridge, Woods set a new record on every lap of the race apart from one; this happened

to be when he had to stop to refuel. Finishing in 3h 25m 25s, his average speed of 77.16 mph for the entire race was, in fact, almost 2 mph faster than Tim Hunt's single lap record from the previous year!

With His Royal Highness Prince George, fourth son of King George V, looking on with great interest, the 1932 Senior was the first Tourist Trophy to be attended by royalty. Jimmy Simpson set the early pace on board the Norton, raising the lap record to 81.50 mph in the process but Woods was always present and was a mere 5 seconds in arrears as he crossed the line to start his third lap. Once more Simpson's luck started to desert him, this time manifesting itself in a failing clutch, and Woods moved into the lead. Holding on to his position as well as he could, Simpson continued to battle round the island to ultimately finish in third place just fourteen seconds behind Norton team mate Jimmy Guthrie. Norton had swept the board with a Royal one-two-three.

Sid Gleave's victory on an Excelsior in

ABOVE Prince George who took an avid interest in the TT

the 1933 Lightweight paled into insignificance compared to the performances of Woods in the Junior and Senior races. Leading from start to finish and setting new lap and race records in both events he was truly unstoppable. Only Tim Hunt could get close in the Junior and a new record on the second lap of the Senior by Jimmie Guthrie was instantly dismissed by Woods as he lapped at 82.69 mph and then at 82.74 mph. For Norton it could not have been better for not only had Woods claimed victory in both classes, he had also led a

factory one-two-three in each with Hunt and Guthrie in the Junior and Simpson and Hunt in the Senior.

Despite having raced at the TT since 1922, Jimmy Simpson had never ridden Lightweight until, in 1934, he teamed up with Graham Walker and Ernie Nott in a privateer team onboard Rudge-Whitworth machines; Rudge themselves having not entered a team due to financial difficulties. Stanley Woods, following a fall out with Norton, was entered on an Italian Moto Guzzi.

Unable to fire up his machine, Simpson was already out of sight of the starter by the time his bike fired into life but despite this inauspicious introduction to the class he was up to fourth place by the end of the first lap as mist hung over the course. On the second circuit it started to rain but Jimmy just seemed to find more speed and was soon in second place behind New Imperial's Charlie Dodson taking the lead as they entered the fourth lap. The crowd, all too aware of Simpson's record for snatching defeat from the jaws of victory, could only hold their breath as the laps ticked down. Could Simpson win a TT on his twenty-fourth attempt? Conditions worsened but there was no

ABOVE Stanley Woods, riding a Norton wins the Junior race

stopping the Brummie as he recorded his fastest lap on the final circuit before taking one of the most popular wins in TT history and a Rudge one-two-three.

In the Junior and Senior events another rider broke his TT duck with a notable pair of wins. Jimmie Guthrie, continuing the Norton domination of the classes, took victory in poor conditions leading Simpson and Nott in the Junior and Simpson and Velocette-mounted Walter Rusk in the Senior.

No Limits!

JIMMIE GUTHRIE REPEATED HIS Junior success in the 1934 TT by leading a Norton clean sweep of the class with team mates Rusk and John White in 1935, but his achievement was overshadowed by that of Stanley Woods who had agreed to ride for Moto Guzzi in both the Lightweight and the Senior; Carlo Guzzi himself had come to observe the Irish Campionissimo at work.

Despite the wet conditions, Woods set off at a blistering pace and took the lap record on the first circuit at 73.68 mph to lead Ernie Nott onboard his Rudge by almost a minute. As the weather closed in further it seemed that Stanley could not help but go faster still and the lap record was broken again, this time at 74.19 mph, despite nearly crashing at Governor's Bridge in the fog. In an astounding ride, only just outside the

CENTRE Spectators watching Stanley Woods riding a Norton as he rounds Governor's Bridge during the Junior race of 1936

race record set in dry and clear conditions, Woods took his sixth TT victory to date and the first for a continental machine.

Great excitement surrounded the Senior and much expectation lay at the feet of Woods and his Guzzi but with a little over a lap remaining the Irishman trailed Guthrie by 26 seconds; surely this was too much to make up on the flying Scot in a single lap? But Woods had already planned for this eventuality. As Guthrie sped past the Grandstand for the last time the Guzzi team were in plain sight preparing for Woods to refuel the thirsty v-twin but Woods had no intention of making the stop having briefed his pitman in advance. Storming across the line to start his final lap Stanley proceeded to put in the lap of his life. When Guthrie crossed the line he was hailed a champion but Woods was still on the course. Crossing the line, just as the press aeroplane was taking off with pictures of Jimmy Guthrie for the morning papers, Woods had recorded a record lap of 85.53 mph. He had beaten his rival by just four seconds to

ABOVE Spectators are advised of the postponement of the 1936 Lightweight due to bad weather

take his greatest ever victory and the Senior/Junior double.

Woods may well have claimed the 1936 double had he not been plagued once more by reliability problems. Riding a German-built DKW, Woods set the early pace in the Lightweight with a record 76.20 mph closely pursued by his team mate Arthur Geiss and Bob Foster on a New Imperial. On the

second lap, plug difficulties caused the German to slow and on the third Woods suffered the same fate allowing Foster to move into the lead. After some roadside repairs Woods was once again in the fight and with an astonishing turn of speed moved himself back into the lead but it was not to last. Just five miles into his penultimate lap Woods' problems returned and a second plug change was

BELOW Riders negotiate Creg-Ny-Baa at high speed during the 1936 TT

required leaving Foster to storm around his final lap to take victory at a record 74.28 mph.

In the Junior class, Norton achieved their sixth consecutive victory as their domination of the class continued through the decade. This time it was the turn of Grimsby's Freddie Frith, riding in his first TT, to take the honours and a new class and lap record. Frith, however, was no stranger to the island having competed in the Manx Grand Prix since 1930, taking a win in the Lightweight Manx in 1935.

As the reigning champion, Woods was first away in the Senior aboard a new rear-spring framed 499cc Velocette but it was Norton-mounted 1935 Junior TT winner Jimmy Guthrie who set the early pace, breaking the lap record on his second circuit to lead Woods by almost half a minute with Frith in third place. As Woods gradually started to close the gap, the Norton team egged their rider on to go faster and this he did, recording yet another record lap at 86.76 mph. But Stanley Woods was not beaten yet and he promptly responded with a phenomenal 86.98 mph lap to close in once again. As Guthrie pulled away from the pits to start his final lap

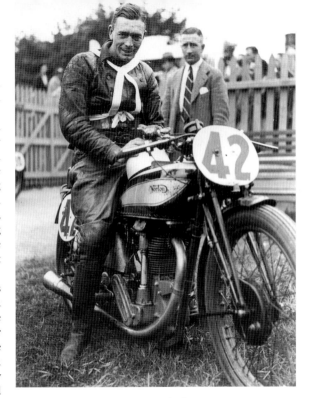

ABOVE Freddie Frith on his Norton

having made a last-minute refuelling stop, the eager spectators knew they were in for an amazing showdown. How much time had Guthrie lost taking on fuel? Both riders rode as hard as they dared in that last lap but it was the undoing of Woods as his machine started to misfire and started to slow. On crossing the finish line the Irishman

could only wait to see if his Scots adversary had done enough. He had but with a margin of just 18 seconds. Guthrie had once again put Norton at the top of the TT podium.

Supported in his efforts by Freddie Frith and John 'Crasher' White and despite the best efforts of Velocette-mounted Woods, Norton pulled off yet another podium 1-2-3 as the Guthrie/Norton partnership paid divi-

dends once more in the 1937 Junior.

The Lightweight saw the return of the Moto Guzzi machines and once again Woods was in the saddle, this time accompanied by Omobono Tenni; a man known affectionately in the British press as 'The Black Devil'! Also entered were the super-fast DKWs of Ewald Kluge, Siegfried Wünsche and Ernie Thomas and the tried and trusted Excelsiors of Tyrell-Smith and Ginger

Woods. Kluge, as expected, set the early pace on the noisy DKW hotly pursued by Woods who, with a second circuit at 76.89 mph, promptly broke the lap record that had been set just seven seconds earlier by a flying Ernie Thomas. Then, just one lap later, the record went again - this time to The Black Devil himself, Omobono Tenni, with a speed of 77.72 mph which moved him up to fourth. Another lap passed and the flying Italian moved into second place behind Woods as Kluge retired with a snapped throttle cable. Could the Guzzi factory pull off a one-two? Sadly it was not to be as Woods' machine first

BELOW Freddie Frith crossing the finishing line at the end of the Senior race, 1937

started to misfire and then expired with broken valve springs on the final lap gifting victory to the popular Italian.

The Senior was all set to be a most exciting affair. Woods was back on the Velocette whilst Tenni remained on a Guzzi. Guthrie, White and Frith were again on the all-conquering Nortons whilst Jock White was set to deafen the entire Manx population with his astounding supercharged BMW. Guthrie, perhaps buoyed by his victory in the Junior, led Woods in the early stages, breaking the lap record twice before being forced to retire on the Mountain with engine problems on his fifth circuit. At this point Woods took up the running but Frith was only seconds behind and on starting the final lap they were level. Woods was first to finish but all he and the anxious crowd could do was wait. Frith streaked across the finish line and the announcement was made: victory to Freddie Frith by 15 seconds. In completing his phenomenal last lap he had set the first ever 90 mph lap of the Isle of Man TT course at 90.27 mph. It was truly a landmark victory.

Sadly, just a fortnight after the close of the 1937 TT, the race lost one of its greatest sons as Jimmy Guthrie lost his life in a terrible crash whilst competing for Norton in the German Grand Prix at Sachsenring. In his honour, a monument was erected on the island at exactly the point on the Mountain where he retired in that last race.

Woods was back on form and back on the Velocette for the 1938 TT and was all but unchallenged in the Junior, winning by a colossal margin of four minutes from team mate Ted Mellor who was locked in a ferocious battle with Freddie Frith on a Norton; so much so that on completing his seven laps it was another 34 miles before someone managed to stop him!

In the Lightweight, Kluge got the win he so richly deserved as he took the DKW to victory with a margin of eleven minutes over Ginger Woods' Excelsior. The Senior, it seemed, was once again run for the benefit of the Norton factory as Harold Daniell led home Freddie Frith and John White with only Stanley Woods able to split the three by taking second place.

The 1939 TT was run in curious circumstances as the spectre of impending war gripped the nation. The Junior was won by Stanley Woods, his tenth TT victory, on a Velocette with a margin of just eight seconds over Harold Daniell, who

OPPOSITE L J Archer at Quarter Bridge

Georg 'Schorsch' Meier and Jock West there was everything to play for as the Senior drew near. Their supercharged 500cc boxer twin was a technological marvel and was reputed to have a top speed in excess of 140 mph – in 1939! The team had, however, been dealt a blow when in practice Austrian Karl Gall had crashed heavily and lost his life.

Meier was running fastest at the end of the first lap with Woods and West inseparable for second place but a disaster struck at half distance when Woods, having pitted for fuel, could not restart his machine. Eventually back in the running he set off in pursuit but was now back in fourth behind the BMW pair and Freddie Frith's privateer Norton, the factory having elected not to send a team due to excessive demands from the War Department. The BMW's were unstoppable in their quest for victory and flew around the island to a creditable one-two for the Bavarian works.

Within a few short months Britain was once again at war and the TT races would have to wait, and an unfortunate few would never get to see the island again.

had unfortunately fallen on the second lap after setting a new record of 85.05 mph, with Heiner Fleischmann of the DKW factory in third. Ted Mellors, having done a better job at remembering how many laps he had completed, won the Lightweight on an Italian Benelli taking the first TT win for the marque from Ewald Kluge's DKW.

With German machines having taken second place in both the Junior and the Lightweight, for the BMW team of

No Limit – The Film.

George Shuttleworth is a dreamer and what he dreams of most is winning the Isle of Man TT race. Having built his own machine, the Shuttleworth Snap, he hopes for a place in the Rainbow race team but is turned down flat. But all is not lost! His mother appropriates his grandfather's nest egg and he's on his way!

Directed by Monty Banks and filmed on location in the Isle of Man during the actual TT races for a budget of £30,000, the film No Limit (1935)

starred one of the most popular comic actors of the day, ukulele playing George Formby, in what is widely regarded as his most popular film of all time. Formby was a great fan of motor-cycles and of the TT itself and needed no further encouragement when approached about making the film which was his first for Associated Talking Pictures.

With love interest supplied by Florence Desmond, a caddish adversary in the form of Jack Hobbs and a catchy score, including the ditty "Riding in the TT Races", the film was an instant hit with the public and is shown during TT week on the Isle of Man to this day!

ABOVE TT rider Richard "Milky" Quayle's replica of the Shuttleworth Snap

LEFT George Formby who starred as George Shuttleworth in the film 'No Limit'

Chapter 5

Norton, Norton, Norton…

TO THE DELIGHT OF THE ISLE OF Man's population, racing returned to the island in the summer of 1946 in the form of the massed start Manx Grand Prix and then in 1947 with the Tourist Trophy. For its renaissance the TT now boasted three new classes: the Lightweight, Junior and Senior Clubman's TT Races on what were ostensibly production machines. The Lightweight and Junior Clubman's retained the traditional 175cc and 250cc capacity limits but machines in the Senior Clubman's were permitted to boast an engine of up to 1000cc – double the existing limit. Bikes were required to be fitted out with all normal road-going accoutrements. Lights,

mudguards, standard exhausts and kickstarts were all obligatory. The races themselves were to be run over a reduced distance of three laps for the Lightweight and four for the Junior and Senior Clubman's with a mandatory pit stop required on completion of the second circuit. The first Clubman's TT attracted an entry of 64 machines but there were, unsurprisingly, doubts over the sagaciousness of allowing club-level amateur riders loose on the Mountain course. And in response it was decided that riders in Clubman's classes would be allocated practice times well away from those of the regular TT riders.

In the TT itself, Velocette dominated the Junior class taking eight out of the

ABOVE A J Bell of Ireland (right) on a Norton and E J Frend on an AJS in action at Quarter Bridge

first twelve places including the first four with Bob Foster, winner of the 1936 Lightweight, victorious with an average speed of 80.31 mph from David Whitworth. The Lightweight, on this occasion run concurrently with the Senior TT, was won by the fantastically named Manliffe Barrington who led home a Moto Guzzi one-two, partnered by Maurice Cann, ahead of the Excelsior of Ben Drinkwater. With Woods enjoying retirement, reigning lap record holder Harold Daniell of the Norton team was expected to clean up in the Senior but Artie Bell, a young Ulsterman riding his first TT, had other ideas as he led the Londoner by four seconds at the end of the first lap.

ABOVE A J Bell of Ireland (right) on a Norton and E J Frend on an AJS in action at Quarter Bridge

year's races due to crashing his Guzzi in practice, took victory in the Junior at the controls of a Velocette from his friend and team mate Bob Foster. Maurice Cann bettered his 1947 second place by taking a second, consecutive victory for the Guzzi factory in the Lightweight. Flying Ulsterman Artie Bell, who had come so close to victory in his battle with Daniell, left all the others trailing in the Senior by winning with a margin of almost eleven minutes from Norton team mate Bill Doran.

In 1949 the Isle of Man TT became recognised as the British round of the newly formed Road Racing World Championship. By this time it was apparent that the Lightweight was fast becoming a Moto Guzzi benefit as factory riders Tommy Wood and Dickie Dale set equal fastest laps at 80.44 mph before team mate Manliffe Barrington took victory by just 12 seconds from Wood. The Freddie Frith/Velocette partnership again won the Junior in what was to be his last TT before retiring after winning the World 350cc Championship later that year.

Artie Bell could only manage fourth in

Daniell fought back and throughout the race the lead changed hands no less than seven times in six laps. Starting the final lap Bell led by a single second and Daniell was once again forced to dig deep into his reserves. In a nail-biting climax he crossed the line with a 22-second advantage over his rival, who had been slowed whilst negotiating slower-moving Junior machines, to take his second TT title.

A familiar name returned to the top of the result sheets in 1948 as Freddie Frith, who had missed the previous

the Senior behind winning Norton team mate Harold Daniell although it had been Bob Foster's Guzzi that had set the fastest lap at just a whisker off of 90 mph. Also of note was a win in the Senior Clubman's for rookie Geoff Duke who, having been denied entry to the 1948 event due to his lack of experience had been accepted to ride on the back of a fine performance in the Manx.

Despite factory rider Maurice Cann setting the early pace in a rare massed-start edition of the race, Guzzi's domination in the Lightweight took a temporary lapse in 1950. Dario Ambrosini, riding a specially prepared Benelli fitted with a long range fuel tank that could last the entire race distance, was in fifth place at the end of the first lap, a minute down on the Guzzi. As the race progressed the young Italian increased his speed and started to close in on the Guzzi until, speeding past the Grandstand with one lap remaining, he was in second place just 15 seconds behind Cann who was, himself, riding like a man possessed. As each mile passed,

Ambrosini edged closer until, after just over three hours of racing, he was on Cann's back wheel. Locked together, with the Guzzi rider using the entire road to defend his position, the two riders stormed over the top of the Mountain. Ambrosini attacked and managed to squeeze past his adversary

BELOW Some of the 4,000 motorcycles waiting to take part in the Senior Event, 1950

but Cann would not relent. Flying down the Glenorutchery Road towards the Grandstand the result seemed too close. The announcement came from the timekeepers that Ambrosini had won by 0.2 seconds, the closest finish in TT history.

Having won the Junior TT on three consecutive years another win for Velocette seemed inevitable, especially with super-fast Bob Foster at the controls but it was Norton-mounted Artie

Bell who charged around the course, leading from start to finish, to take the victory. Bell's average speed of 86.33 mph for the race distance was, in fact, faster than the existing lap record set by Freddie Frith some thirteen years before.

The Senior was also a one-man show as Geoff Duke, now a member of Norton's 'A' team, set a new lap record of 93.01 mph on his first circuit, raising this to 93.33 mph on his second.

BELOW The position board in the 1950 TT

Unchallenged, Duke sped around the island's roads to cross the finish line abreast with team mate Artie Bell who had started his TT two minutes and forty seconds before him.

1951 saw a revamped Ultra-Lightweight class for 125cc machines introduced with honours in the two-lap sprint being taken by Irishman Cromie McCandless on a DOHC Mondial at 73.34 mph – a speed that could have won a Senior TT just twenty years earlier. The Ultra-Lightweight had been a very successful first TT outing for the Italian Mondial factory with their machines finishing in the top four places over seven minutes clear of the nearest opposition.

There was a return to business as usual in the Lightweight class with Moto Guzzi taking top honours. Benelli rider Dario Ambrosini once again fought a pitched battle but carburettor problems prevented the Italian from making a clean pass allowing the Guzzi of Tommy Wood to take the win by just eight seconds.

Geoff Duke built upon his 1950 success by taking wins in both the Junior and Senior TT. Run in perfect conditions, Duke led the Junior from the start, setting a new record on his first circuit of the island in true Stanley Woods style before breaking it again on the second lap at an amazing 91.38 mph. Unchallenged throughout, Geoff

ABOVE Geoff Duke and Artie Bell race for the finishing line, 1950

was able to ease back but still finish three minutes clear of team mates Johnny Lockett and Jack Brett. In the Senior, Duke led Lockett by forty seconds at the end of the first lap and, in trademark fashion, broke the lap record on his second circuit at 95.22 mph. Duke continued to push on and, as many of his rivals fell by the wayside with mechanical difficulties, went on to win by over four minutes from AJS rider Bill Doran with Ultra-Lightweight champion Cromie McCandless in third place on a privateer Norton.

Another Italian manufacturer, MV Agusta, took victory in the Ultra-Lightweight at the 1952 TT with Cecil Sandford at the controls ahead of the three factory Mondials of Carlo Ubbiali, Len Parry and McCandless. Moto Guzzi domination of the Lightweight continued thanks to the efforts of winner, Fergus Anderson, and team mates Enrico Lorenzetti and Syd Lawton.

The offer of a factory ride from the Italian Gilera concern had not tempted Duke in the year that had passed since his Senior/Junior double so once again he took to the start line aboard the unstoppable Norton. Untroubled by rider or mechanical difficulties, his second consecutive victory in the Junior appeared to be a mere formality albeit without a new lap record. In the Senior, Duke set the pace from the start despite an intermittent misfire problem but, with clutch problems nearing the end of the fourth lap, he was forced to retire. The Senior was won by his team mate, Reg Armstrong, despite the fact that his chain broke the very second he crossed the finish line!

MV Agusta & Moto Guzzi repeated their 1953 victories with honours going to Les Graham in the Ultra-Lightweight and Anderson, taking his second consecutive title, in the Lightweight. Nine of the twelve finishers in the 125cc event were, in fact, from the MV Factory.

With Geoff Duke a non-starter in the Junior, having at last moved from the Norton factory which he now considered uncompetitive to that of Gilera, the race was once again a wide open concern. Leading from start to finish the race was won by a relative newcomer to the Isle of Man; Rhodesian Ray Amm on a 350cc works Norton!

The Senior was set to be an altogether different affair as Duke took to the start line on the powerful 'Nortonised'

BELOW Geoff Duke being congratulated on his victory in 1950

Gilera – so called because of the amount of input that Geoff had put into its development and refinement. Another Duke victory was expected by all as he set a new absolute lap record of 97.20 mph on his second circuit, however, one rider had not read the script; Ray Amm who promptly bettered Duke's record with a 97.41 mph lap of his own. Duke knew he had a race on his hands! As Amm pitted before his fourth lap Duke rode straight through, determined to distance himself from the pretender to his throne but, pushing the Gilera to its limit, he lost control on a patch of wet tar exiting Quarter Bridge. The slide and resulting crash had split Duke's fuel tank, spilling all his fuel onto the road.

BELOW A combination rounding a bend of the Clypse course in the reinstated 500cc Sidecar class

With that his race was over leaving Amm free to take the Junior/Senior double with his team mate Jack Brett in second place.

A new circuit, the Clypse Course, was introduced to the TT in 1954 for use in the Ultra-Lightweight and the newly reinstated 500cc Sidecar Class. Already popular as a bicycle racing course it started opposite the Grandstand in the same place as the full Mountain circuit before turning right towards Willaston Corner and on to Cronk-Ny-Mona and on to Creg-Ny-Baa. From here riders forked right down Ballacarrooin Hill and on to Hall Corner and Onchan before heading back via Signpost Corner and Governor's Bridge to the Grandstand – a total of 10.79 miles.

The first event to be held on the new course was the 10-lap Ultra-Lightweight. A close race ensued between the MV of Carlo Ubbiali and the NSU of Rupert Hollaus, the verdict going to the German with a margin of four seconds. Back on the Mountain course and in an upset to the norm, MV Agusta could only manage fifth place in the Lightweight as the NSU factory continued to dominate the top placings with the win going to Werner Haus

and NSUs filling the next four places.

As if to prove that his win was no fluke, Amm repeated his Senior win the following year, relegating Geoff Duke to second place more than a minute behind as the race was cut short to four laps due to terrible weather conditions. By setting a record lap of 94.61 mph aboard the hi-tech, streamlined Proboscis Norton in the Junior, another double appeared on the cards but with less than a lap to go an engine failure put paid to his hopes, allowing a surprise victory to be taken by AJS rider Rod Coleman.

ABOVE Geoff Duke (right) receiving the trophy for Sportsman of the Year, 1953

Chapter 6

Forza Italia!

WITH NSU HAVING OFFICIALLY withdrawn from all racing activities, the stage was once again set for the Italian factories to dominate the lightweight classes at the 1955 TT. Debuting on the island, Switzerland's Luigi Taveri led the field on his fully-faired MV through the early laps on the Clypse circuit until he was caught and passed at just over half distance by his team mate Carlo Ubbiali. However, Taveri would not let Ubbiali slip away and briefly took the lead once more on the final lap before being passed again by the flying Italian at Creg-ny-Baa who held on to take victory in Douglas by just two seconds.

More changes were afoot in the Lightweight, not only through the absence of the Germans but also because it too had been moved to the smaller Clypse circuit. Moto Guzzi's Cecil Sandford lead for seven of the

nine laps before being passed at Ballacoar Corner by MV's Bill Lomas who finished in first place almost a minute clear of the Guzzi.

Having accepted 125cc and 250cc rides for MV Agusta, Lomas was informed by AJS that they no longer required his services in the Junior and Senior races, however, to his good fortune the 1953 Lightweight winner Fergus Anderson came to the rescue and

charge, eventually taking an unassailable lead on the fifth lap to finish exactly a minute clear.

The 1955 Senior was set to be an exciting affair but it was to start without reigning champion Ray Amm who had tragically been killed during his first race of the season riding an MV at Imola. Geoff Duke took the lead on the first lap ahead of his Gilera team mate Reg Armstrong and the Moto Guzzi of Ken Kavanagh. Then followed the news that Duke had lapped the island in 22m 39s – 100 mph! A great cheer erupted from the Grandstand but it was premature. A second announcement came through: 99.97 mph. It was so very close but it was, nevertheless, not 100mph. Oblivious to the fuss, Duke pressed on and gradually pulled clear of his opposition and, despite having to contain a frightening 136 mph slide at full lock, he finished two minutes clear of Armstrong with a record speed of 97.93 mph. Lomas had finished in seventh place;

BELOW An MV Augusta, 1956

offered Bob his 350cc and 500cc Moto Guzzi rides. In the Junior, Glaswegian Bob 'Mac' McIntyre led the race after the first lap on his aerodynamic Joe Potts-prepared Norton closely pursued by John Surtees, Cecil Sandford and a fast Bob Lomas who by the end of lap two had moved up into second place as he got used to riding the unfamiliar Guzzi. Mac continued to set a blistering pace but Lomas was unrelenting in his

not an astounding achievement in itself but in doing so he became the first rider to finish four TTs in a single week.

With the Italian factories reigning supreme in the solos and the BMW-pairing of Schneider and Strauss taking the 500cc Sidecar title, it had been an abysmal week for the British manufacturers with not one of their machines taking victory outside of the Clubman's events. But, unbeknownst to them their troubles were just beginning.

The conditions were appalling at the start of the 1956 Lightweight as the heavens opened and the rain flooded down. In a massed start it was Sammy Miller aboard a privateer NSU Sport-Max who set the early pace, completing his first lap six seconds ahead of Ubbiali and his MV team mate, Roberto Columbo, who was a further thirty seconds behind. Miller continued to ride a fantastic race but, as the rain eased, the Italian took advantage and slipped into the lead. Undeterred the Belfastman gave chase but it was too much for his machine and as the pair reached the top of the long, fast climb to Creg-ny-Baa the engine seized leaving Ubbiali clear to take victory by over two minutes.

That very afternoon the Ultra-

RIGHT Carlo Ubbiali competing in the Ultra Lightweight event, 1956

Lightweight was scheduled and with entries from the Spanish Montesa, Czechoslovakian CZ and Italian Mondial and MV factories it promised to be an exciting affair. Once again Ubbiali was bettered at the start, this time by the Mondial of Cecil Standford and by the end of the first lap he was sixteen seconds in arrears but Ubbiali was a rider who relished a challenge and on the fifth lap he stole past going into the sharp corner at Creg-ny-Baa. Stanford gave chase but, as with Miller in the previous race, he soon retired with engine problems. Ubbiali charged on to take victory and a 125/250cc double for MV.

With the Gilera banned from participating for supporting a riders' strike at the Dutch GP, many predicted a repeat victory for Bill Lomas in the Junior. Mounted on a powerful Guzzi he blasted around the wet first lap, sliding his way through the corners, with John Surtees in pursuit on a thundering four-cylinder MV. Lomas looked unstoppable but as he climbed out of Ramsey on the Mountain road for the sixth time his engine blew forcing retirement. Surtees took over control but by now, having been over a minute down,

Lomas's team mate Ken Kavanagh was moving fast through the field – so much so that at the start of the final lap Surtees' lead was half a second. Then disaster struck as, with a cough and a splutter, Surtees' MV ran out of fuel leaving the way open for Kavanagh to take victory having averaged 89.29 mph for the race.

Surtees made up for his Junior disappointment in the Senior TT. Leading from start to finish on his MV he was never once challenged for supremacy. His victory is perhaps a little more unusual in that he was forced to start the race on his spare bike having written off his number-one machine in practice after colliding with… a cow!

The Clubman's classes were abandoned in 1957 so the programme was back to four races for solo machines and one for the sidecars as the Tourist

ABOVE John Surtees

ABOVE Bob McIntyre riding a Gilera in the Senior 500cc event, June 1957

Trophy celebrated its Golden Jubilee. Once again the Italian machines dominated. Cecil Standford buried old ghosts by winning the Lightweight over an increased distance of ten laps on his Mondial bettering MV's Luigi Taveri by almost two minutes; his team mate, Tarquinio Provini, having been forced to retire after setting the fastest lap with Ubbiali also a non-finisher. Provini made up for his difficulties in the Ultra-Lightweight by working his way through the field following a poor start to take the lead and the victory from an unlucky Ubbiali.

Bob McIntyre started the Junior on a new four-cylinder 350cc Gilera that could scream its way to a 145 mph top speed but was, in itself, a heavy machine weighing almost half as much again as the svelte works Guzzi. Mac blitzed away from the start line to take a substantial lead of forty-one seconds at the end of the first circuit and a new lap record. But the usually reliable Gilera hit a problem and started missing on one cylinder forcing McIntyre to slow, allowing Guzzi's Dickie Dale into the lead closely pursued by privateer Norton-rider John Hartle. But their lead did not last. Hartle, nearing Sulby at the north of the circuit, rounded Quarry Bends and hit a patch of oil dumped by one of the other machines. He was instantly thrown off. Before anybody could offer a warning Dale thundered into the corner and suffered the same fate. All the two riders could do was to pull their machines to the side and spectate. Whilst this was occurring Bob Mac had stopped his machine at the roadside and changed an errant plug. Back in business and on all four cylinders he retook the lead and sped home to victory.

An enormous amount was expected of McIntyre as he lined up for the start of the Senior and he failed to disappoint in what was an historic ride. Tearing away from the line on the big Gilera he posted a first-lap speed of 99.99 mph to break the lap record from a standing start. But then he went better still as on his second circuit he posted 101.03 mph. The magic 100 mph barrier had been broken! On the fourth lap the record fell yet again; this time at 101.12 mph. Then,

after a stop to refuel, the Scotsman came within a whisker of disaster when a stone flew up from the rear wheel of a back marker and struck a startled McIntyre on the forehead just below his helmet. Although racked with pain he amazingly managed to maintain control before pushing on and catching John Surtees on the same lap. Mac then slowed and allowed the MV to pass him comfortable in the knowledge that he only had to keep Surtees in sight to

LEFT Bob McIntyre astride his Gilera

guarantee victory. As the two riders crossed the line together Mac knew he had ridden the race of his life ensuring his place in TT folklore for ever more.

To the surprise and shock of the racing community, Mondial, Moto Guzzi and Gilera all announced at the end of the 1957 that, due to the escalating costs involved, they would no longer be supporting factory racing teams. Only the personal intervention of Count

Agusta prevented MV from going the same way.

Ubbiali led the field during the early laps of the 1958 Lightweight aboard his MV while hot on his tail was team mate Tarquinio Provini, who had defected from Mondial. At the end of the fourth lap Provini made his move and took the lead. Refusing to wait for Ubbiali, Provini upped the pace and the two raced all the way to the line putting on a

BELOW Bob McIntyre leading John Surtees at Governor's Corner during the 1957 Senior TT

fantastic show for the crowds with his rival losing out by a mere eight seconds. In third place on an NSU was a TT rookie by the name of Mike Hailwood whose name would soon become synonymous with the whole concept of the Isle of Man TT.

At the end of the first lap of the Ultra-Lightweight, Luigi Taveri led the field on the all new desmodromic valve 125cc Ducati closely tracked by the MVs of Provini and Ubbiali but it was not to last as on the fourth lap Taveri's machine experienced engine problems forcing him to pull to the side of the road at Creg-ny-Baa. Within half a lap Provini was also in trouble having crashed his machine at Nursery Bends. It was just left to Ubbiali to hold off the charging Ducati of Romolo Ferri – a task he performed superbly to take his third Ultra-Lightweight title and another victory for the MV factory.

In the Junior TT, MV had a great deal of hope for their two riders but all did not immediately go to plan as a faulty

with mechanical problems of his own leaving Surtees to storm home four minutes clear of the field. Victory number three for MV!

The Senior TT went much the same way as Surtees led from start to finish with a fastest lap in excess of 100 mph while McIntyre once again retired with engine trouble and Hartle, who had himself lapped at the magic ton, crashed at Governor's Bridge, his bike bursting into flames and burning out at the roadside. Surtees had taken the coveted Senior/Junior double and in doing so secured MV their fourth title at

piston sidelined Hartle at the Bungalow on the first lap. Surtees took control of the race but McIntyre looked ever the threat as he tracked the super-fast MV on his Norton. Fortunately for MV their luck changed on the second lap as an unfortunate Mac was forced to retire

the 1958 TT and a clean sweep of the results.

MV's TT domination extended to the following year. Tarquinio Provini proved that he was the undisputed king of the Clypse Course in its last year of use by once again taking the

Lightweight title and adding to it the Ultra-Lightweight. Both were tremendously close tussles right to the line with Provini beating MZ's Taverni by seven seconds in the 250cc race and team mate Ubbiali by point four of a second in the 125cc – the smallest winning margin in the history of TT racing.

In the Junior TT, John Surtees led the field from start to finish and was never once troubled on his way to a three-minute victory over his MV team mate John Hartle who had fought hard to hold off the constant attacks of Norton's Alistair King.

The Senior, having been postponed a day due to poor weather, was a war of attrition not just between riders but against the elements too. Starting in fine weather, Surtees stormed away from the line to set a new absolute lap record of 101.18 mph pursued by Hartle and McIntyre, who had been forced to retire from the Junior with mechanical problems. But the fair-weather start soon gave way to howling winds and, in a moment, a thick fog had descended across the upland roads and the Mountain making visibility a problem and the roads damp and greasy. Hartle came down heavily as his bike slipped

from underneath him at Glen Vine on the road to Ballacraine as gradually more riders retired. The weather deteriorated further as hail began to fall but the organisers made no attempt to call off the race. After the seven hardest laps of his racing career, Surtees crossed the line as winner – his hands frozen to the bars, his machine all but stripped of paint. It was an astounding achievement but one that he never wanted to go through again! With that win Surtees had equalled Stanley Woods' Senior/Junior doubles record and for a second year secured a clean sweep for MV of the principal classes.

Another pair of Solo class was held during the 1959 TT but scrapped immediately afterwards. The Formula 1 races were designed for production machines and run over three laps of the Mountain circuit. Bob McIntyre was victorious in the 500cc class with the 350cc won by Alistair King.

Also present at the 1959 TT was a highly organised and professional team from Japan: Honda. With a squad that had never left Japanese shores they were in the Isle of Man not to win but to learn and the next few years would prove that they were fast learners indeed!

Chapter 7

Ago, Mike and the Japanese

WITH MASSED STARTS ABANDONED and both Lightweight classes reverting to the full Mountain circuit, the 1960 TT took on a shape that would last through to the present day.

For a third consecutive year the MV factory dominated proceedings. Carlo Ubbiali repeated his 1958 form to win the Ultra-Lightweight from team mates Gary Hocking and Luigi Taveri in a race that demonstrated the rapid progression of Honda; the Japanese factory taking sixth to eleventh, ahead of the Pagani's MV and the Ducatis of Jim Redman and Dave Clark. Welsh-born Rhodesian Hocking went one better in the Lightweight swapping placings with Ubbiali in another MV one-two ahead of the Morini of Tarquinio Provini.

Eighty riders lined up for the start of a Junior race which once again saw John Surtees speed away from the line to set a record time on his first lap with fellow MV rider John Hartle in second place and Bob McIntyre in third. With a lap of 99.2 mph under his belt it looked as if the first Junior 100 mph lap was on the cards but a problem with his gear selector was causing Surtees to slow and gradually Hartle and Mac were closing in. Lap-by-lap Hartle got ever closer until, as he sped through Sulby on his fifth lap of six, he took the lead, first on time and then on the road

to take victory by over two minutes.

Putting the disappointment of the Junior result behind him, Surtees' performance in the Senior was outstanding. Recording a 103.03 mph lap from a standing start and improving that to 104.08 mph on his second circuit he was unstoppable. Hailwood, Hartle and Minter all lapped in excess of the ton, Minter the first rider to do so on a single-cylinder machine. On crossing the line, having lapped at an average speed of 102.44 mph, Surtees had equalled Stanleys Woods' achievement of four Senior titles and handed MV their third consecutive clean sweep of the solo honours.

Honda's patience finally paid off. Whereas their 1959 team had comprised almost entirely of inexperienced

ABOVE Mike Hailwood at his peak

Bray Hill and onto Quarter Bridge the man from Oxfordshire seemed unstoppable on his way to setting a new lap record pursued by Taveri, Phillis et al. Taveri then went faster still but Hailwood never once let the pace slip on the way to his first TT victory just eight seconds ahead of the Italian to the delight of company founder Soichiro Honda; his advanced and nimble machines had taken the first five places.

Later that same day Hailwood was back on a Honda: this time the four-cylinder 250cc RC162 alongside Phillis, Redman and 'Flying Scot' Bob McIntyre. Mac broke the lap record on his opening lap to lead the field by some twenty-five seconds. On his second circuit he went faster still as Hailwood moved into second place ahead of Rhodesian Gary Hocking on the MV. McIntyre powered on but his machine could not make the distance and on the final lap his engine seized leaving Hailwood to take his second win with Honda once more enjoying a top five clean sweep

Bob Mac's luck was no better in the Junior. Riding an Italian works Bianchi he briefly led the field but was forced to retire as his gearbox failed on the first lap

domestic riders their 1961 TT squad contained the glitterati of Lightweight racers: Mike Hailwood, Jim Redman, Luigi Taveri, Tom Phillis and the Japanese aces Sadao Shimizaki and Naomi Taniguchi. Aboard a 125cc RC142, Hailwood was waved off by the timekeepers. Screaming his way down

leaving the race open for 22-year-old Phil Read to take his Norton to victory and the first win for a British-built bike in the premier classes for seven years.

With Honda not having a big-cc race bike, Hailwood started the Senior on board a Norton as did McIntyre, Phillis and Read. On the first lap Hocking was in control, leading Hailwood by less than half a minute, but he could not maintain the storming pace as gradually his MV slipped back through the field before he was forced to retire. Hailwood, however, had his head down and was on a charge. Constantly lapping in excess of 100 mph, nothing could

LEFT Bob McIntyre cornering on his Honda during the Lightweight 250cc event, June 1961

stop him on his way to his third historic victory of the week.

Honda maintained their good fortune in the 1962 TT, taking twin victories with Taveri at last taking a TT victory in the Ultra-Lightweight and Kent's Derek Minter the Lightweight. In the Junior Hailwood scored yet another win with a margin of just five seconds from team mate Hocking whilst Bob Mac was once again forced to retire with

mechanical problems in what was to be his last TT.

The Senior race saw Hailwood and Hocking line up once again on the big MVs. Hocking was untroubled throughout the entire race winning with an almost ten-minute margin from Norton's Ellis Boyce as Hailwood suffered mechanical problems. However, his victory was sadly overshadowed by the tragic death of his great friend,

BELOW Pushing his motorbike to the limit, Derek Minter flashes past the camera on his way to winning the 1962 Lightweight

Australian Tom Phillis, who had crashed heavily at Laurel Bank during the Junior TT. Shocked by this, Hocking never raced motorcycles again.

What occurred over the next five years was nothing short of amazing. Never in the history of the TT had two riders been so central in shaping the results year after year.

A new 50cc class was added to the TT for 1963 with victory going to the diminutive Mitsui Itoh. The Ultra-Lightweight was won by Hugh Anderson who lead home a one-two-three for TT newcomers Suzuki aboard their innovative 125cc disc-valve machine. The Lightweight and Junior classes were both taken in decisive fashion by Honda-riding British-born Rhodesian Jim Redman who became the first rider to push the Junior lap record past the 100 mph barrier. The Senior result was no less decisive as MV's ace Mike Hailwood romped home well over a minute clear of the Gilera of John Hartle.

Anderson added to his 1963 Ultra-Lightweight victory by winning the 1964 50cc title ahead of the Honda of Ralph Bryans while the Ultra-Lightweight itself saw a return to form of 1962 champion Luigi Taveri who was once again contracted to the Honda factory. In a carbon copy of the previous year's results, Jim Redman took victory in the Lightweight and Junior categories whilst Hailwood scored his third Senior title.

Despite setting the fastest lap in the Ultra-Lightweight, there was no TT victory for Anderson's Suzuki in 1964 as he was pushed into second place in the 50cc by the Honda of Taveri who was himself relegated to the runner-up spot in the Ultra-Lightweight by Yamaha's Phil Read. Normality reigned in the Lightweight and Junior classes as the popular Jim Redman pulled off the

MV and headed back onto the circuit, oil leaking, with flattened exhausts and no screen. After an extended pit stop he was back in the race and went on to win by 2m 19s from the Norton of Joe Dunphy.

With Redman sidelined due to a horrific crash in the wet at Spa, Agostini made up for his previous foibles by taking victory in the 1966 Junior with a margin of over ten minutes from the AJS of Peter Williams. Bill Ivy meanwhile took top honours in the Lightweight. Hailwood, having left MV for Honda with the promise of the new RC181, won both the Lightweight with a record speed of 101.79 mph and the Senior having posted a fastest lap at an amazing 107.07 mph.

double for the third consecutive year to the delight of the crowd. In the Senior, Hailwood was joined on the MV team by 22-year-old Giacomo Agostini. Despite the wet conditions and lack of experience on the Mountain circuit young Ago went for it guns blazing only to crash on his second lap at Sarah's Cottage. One lap later Hailwood crashed at exactly the same spot but undeterred he remounted his battered

Stuart Graham led a Suzuki one-two-three aboard the tiny-twin in the1967 50cc but lost out by just four seconds in the Ultra-Lightweight to Phil Read who had returned to the form he had shown in 1965. Mike Hailwood took the Lightweight class with a comfortable margin over Read with a new lap record and average race speed – a feat he repeated in the Junior, taking victory from his MV rival Giacomo Agostini by over three minutes. Once more, production classes returned to the TT with races for 250, 500 and 750cc machines.

The battle for the Senior title was set to be a closer affair with Hailwood on the vicious RC181 and Ago on the similarly matched MV-500. With his machine refusing to start, Hailwood was forced to set off last on the road as Ago stormed round the island to a new lap record. But, as the laps progressed, 'Mike the Bike' steadily chipped away at his rival's advantage, setting a new absolute record of 108.77 mph on his third circuit. But then, to Hailwood's horror, the Honda's twist grip started to work its way loose. Dashing into the pits the team worked frantically to remedy the problem and after 44 seconds he was back on the road. To many it seemed the damage was already done but Mike continued to push on, taking the lead as he passed through Ramsey on his fifth lap. Ago briefly retook the lead but, with incredible bad luck, his chain broke as he rounded Windy Corner leaving Hailwood to ride his sixth and final lap uncontested to once again take three TT titles in a single week.

With twelve TT titles under his belt, 1967 was to be Hailwood's last year on bikes as the lure of four-wheels and a drive in Formula 1 beckoned. But the public hadn't yet seen the last of 'Mike the Bike'.

With Hailwood occupied elsewhere, there was at last an opportunity for Giacomo Agostini to shine. And shine he did, first by taking the Senior/Junior double in 1968 and then again in '69, '70 and '72, only slipping up in 1971 when he could only manage to secure the Senior title due to uncharacteristic reliability problems with his 350cc MV Agusta. For a while it seemed as if his Senior campaign would end in disappointment as his pit crew struggled for over two minutes attempting to rectify a carburetion problem, however, such was Ago's domination on the road that once back on board he still managed to race his way to victory with a margin of over five minutes from the Matchless of Peter Williams. There was, however, a sad conclusion to this period of glory; following the death of Ago's close friend Gilberto Parlotti, who collided with a concrete post on the Mountain during the 1972 Ultra-Lightweight, the Italian Campionissimo declared that he would never race on the Isle of Man again. His boycott would in later years have a great impact on the organisation of the TT.

The 1968 Ultra-Lightweight and Lightweight titles were taken by Yamaha's Phil Read and Bill Ivy whilst Barry Smith took the 50cc title aboard his Derbi in what was to be the last running of the class which had never fully captured the imagination of the manufacturers or riders.

A year later the Ultra-Lightweight was taken by Dave Simmonds aboard a Kawasaki ahead of Kel Carruthers on an Aermacchi. Kel went one better in the Lightweight by taking victory by over three minutes from Suzuki's Frank Peris aboard his Italian Benelli machine. In the production classes, Tony Rogers took a notable win on a 250cc Ducati to score the first TT victory for the Italian marque.

Carruthers repeated his success at the 1970 Lightweight whilst victory in the Ultra-Lightweight went to Germany's Dieter Braun's Suzuki. Yamaha riders Phil Read and Chas Mortimer took the honours in the Lightweight and Ultra-Lightweight, a feat they would reproduce at the TT in 1972.

OPPOSITE Giacomo Agostini in hot pursuit of Mike Hailwood

Chapter 8

Troubled Times

THE 1970S WOULD PROVE TO BE A difficult decade for the Isle of Man TT. For a number of years there had been concerns regarding the speeds attained by the machines and the relative lack of safety on the course, and these misgivings were about to come to a head. Following Parlotti's death at the 1972 TT, Giacomo Agostini had declared he would never race on the Isle of Man again, citing that his only reason for competing was the need for World Championship points. To his mind the Championship would be better served if the TT were removed and replaced with an event on a shorter circuit such as Donington or Silverstone. Ago was not alone as soon Phil Read and Bob Gould joined the cause. Could the TT survive without its greatest stars?

It was all change on the result board as the TT moved into 1973. Tommy

RIGHT Phil Read

Robb led the Yamaha domination of the Ultra-Lightweight as the Japanese manufacturer secured the first four places with ease. This was nothing compared to the result for the 250cc Lightweight. Charlie Williams took victory by twenty-four seconds over (unrelated) John Williams in an astonishing result that saw all-conquering Yamaha TZ250s take the first twenty-nine places.

Yamaha's success was also present in the Junior as Tony Rutter, the father of Superbike star Michael, took victory aboard the two-stroke TZ350 with twenty-second placed Brian Moses aboard an Aermacchi being the first non-Yamaha rider home. It was, however Suzuki Italia-sponsored Jack Findlay on a water-cooled TR500 who beat all opposition to take the Senior title, distancing the Matchless of Peter Williams by well over a minute.

If the 1973 result hadn't been enough to convince the masses of Yamaha's domination, 1974 certainly did as the marque achieved a clean sweep of all the non-production categories with Clive Horton victorious in the Ultra-

ABOVE Pat Hennen riding in the Senior race. He crashed in this race after striking a bird and suffered head injuries so severe that he was forced to retire from the sport

Lightweight, Charlie Williams in the Lightweight, Tony Rutter for a second time in the Junior and Phil Carpenter in the Senior.

For 1975 the racing classes were once again given a shake up. The 125cc Ultra-Lightweight was dropped after twenty-four years and the three production classes were amalgamated into a single class. A new class was added: the Classic 1000cc.

Yamaha dominated the Lightweight and Junior through the efforts of Chas Mortimer and Charlie Williams. Mick Grant, riding the brutal two-stroke triple Kawasaki KR750, fought race long with the Yamaha of John Williams in the Senior to take victory by thirty-one seconds. It was, however, in the Classic that he made history; when forced to retire with a broken chain he had already set a fastest lap on his second circuit of 109.82 mph to crack Hailwood's 1967 absolute lap record.

Still riding the TZ350, Tony Rutter posted an outstanding fastest lap in the 1976 Junior of 108.69 mph, to beat Hailwood's ten-year-old record but ultimately he was denied overall victory by the consistency of Chas Mortimer's Yamaha which finished less than seven seconds in front of him. Many expected Suzuki GP rider John Williams to take an easy victory in the Senior, equipped as he was with the latest technology and all the support of a factory racer. Indeed, this appeared to be the case as he stormed away from the line to break the lap record on his first and second circuits at an astonishing 112.27 mph. But, on the final lap and with an advantage of five minutes, disaster struck as his hi-tech RG500 stalled negotiating the tight corner at Governor's Bridge and could not be re-started – he was out of fuel. In desperation he grabbed hold of the bars and, to the cheers of the crowd, started to push the final half a mile to the finish line. Try as he might, it was not enough. Despite his best efforts he finished in seventh place two-and-a-half minutes down on eventual winner Tom Herron who had no idea he was riding for victory until he saw Williams pushing his immobilized machine. As consolation, Williams made up for his disap-

pointment by taking victory in the Classic 1000cc with a fastest lap of 110.21 mph.

The closed season between 1976 and 1977 was a landmark period for the TT. Under pressure from some riders and manufacturers, and with the series itself constantly under development, a decision was taken to strike the Isle of Man TT from the FIM World Championship. Would the TT survive if the big names and manufacturers were no longer required to be there? Many said it wouldn't but time has proved other-

OPPOSITE Joey Dunlop on a Honda takes a corner, 1978

BELOW John Williams riding a works Honda down Bray Hill. Williams eventually finished second after Mike Hailwood, 1978

wise, although there were to be bad times before the good returned.

With the changes came a new format yet again as the Lightweight and Production were dropped in favour of three new TT Formula classes. Phil Read took a fantastic double by winning both the Formula 1 and the Senior TT whilst Mick Grant made up for his 1975 misfortune by taking the 1000cc Classic. In addition to the regular programme, a one-off four-lap race was run in honour of the Queen's Silver Jubilee, the winner of which was a twenty-five-year-old from Ballymoney in Northern Ireland by the name of William Joseph Dunlop – Joey to his friends.

Tom Heron's five-minute Senior win over Suzuki team mate Billy Guthrie paled into insignificance at the 1978 TT due to the result of the Formula 1. 'Mike the Bike' was back! Riding Steve Wynne's 864cc Ducati twin, Hailwood took on the all-conquering Honda of

ABOVE Mike Hailwood leading Joey Dunlop down Mountain Road. Hailwood later won the race with Dunlop failing to finish, 1978

GP star John Williams to win by two minutes in an emotional victory. Those who thought this would just be a one-off were proved wrong the following year as Hailwood went one better to take the Senior on a Suzuki ahead of Tony Rutter and Denis Ireland with a new lap record of 114.02 mph.

Following the Senior there was still the matter of the Classic which had been billed as "the richest race in the world" with a prize fund of £30,000.

Hailwood was once again on form but so was Scotsman Alex George on a 998cc factory Honda. The two matched each other for the entire race distance as the lead constantly changed hands. Hailwood bettered his lap record to 114.18 mph but it was George who took the verdict by less than four seconds. Standing on the rostrum at the awards presentation Hailwood announced that this time he really was retiring. What better way to be remembered.

Chapter 9

The Road to Recovery

DESPITE THE CONCERNS OF THE organisers that the loss of World Championship status would sound a death knell for the TT, the riders and the fans continued to arrive on Manx shores each year. Even the manufacturers were once again showing a keen interest with the Formula 1 event providing an ideal shop window for production machinery.

The 1980 TT saw amiable New Zealander Graeme Crosby take victory in the Senior as part of the Suzuki Factory squad and Honda Britain's Mick Grant placed first in the Formula 1 but it was the efforts of Joey Dunlop in the Classic that are most remembered. Riding a hybrid machine (Suzuki-derived Seeley chassis, Yamaha engine, a modified fuel tank with an extra section welded in and an undersized screen), Dunlop set off around the circuit at a blistering pace only to have the straps that held his oversized and overweight fuel tank snap. Undeterred he battled on holding the tank in place with his knees. But the enormous 36-litre tank, so nearly his

BELOW Graeme Crosby on his way to a controversial victory in the 1981 Formula 1 TT

undoing, became his saviour as Grant's Honda pit crew struggled with two refuelling stops Joey just needed the one and the time saved combined with a record 115.22 mph final lap secured him victory. Not bad for a privateer on a funny bike from Ballymoney.

It was all change at the top as the circus arrived for the 1981 TT. Mick Grant had left Honda to join Crosby at Suzuki whilst Honda had signed up the talented Dunlop (if you can't beat him, sign him!) to partner Alex George and 'Rocket' Ron Haslam. Ducati-mounted Tony Rutter pulled out a decisive victory over the Honda of Phil Odlin in the Formula 2, setting a new lap record of 103.51 mph in the process, and Grant rode two and a half minutes clear in a Senior cut short by appalling weather conditions on the mountain but controversy surrounded the Formula 1 and the Classic.

Crosby, having been delayed at the start due to a last-minute wheel change, was permitted to set off at the back of the field. Initially Haslam was declared the winner but a protest was lodged by Suzuki's Martyn Ogbourne who argued that no time adjustment had been made for Crosby's delayed start. The Kiwi had

ABOVE Joey Dunlop takes part in Honda Britain's 'Black Friday' protest at the 1981 TT

in fact set a new lap record of 113.70 mph and completed the race distance two minutes faster than Rocket Ron. The appeal was upheld and Haslam was demoted to second place with Crosby declared the winner. But the controversy did not end there as the Honda Britain team, with their noses put out of joint, had something special planned.

As Haslam, Dunlop and George took to the start line for the classic, gone was the red, white and blue of the Honda team – replaced with all black leathers devoid of advertising and black-painted motorcycles in what was to become

known as the Black Friday protest. But,
to Honda's further embarrassment, it
was once again Crosby who took the
victory with team mate Mick Grant in
second place as Haslam retired with
ignition troubles and Dunlop, despite
setting the fastest lap, first ran out of
fuel and then, after having pushed his
machine to the pits for a top up, broke
his cam chain whilst chasing hard to
regain lost time.

The 1982 TT, run under more amica-
ble circumstances, allowed Haslam to
acquire his somewhat overdue TT victory in the Formula 1. Grant had set the
early pace despite having suffered problems with a fading front brake but, on
the fourth lap and with a lead of thirty
seconds, his Suzuki suffered a major oil
leak and he was forced to retire at
Ramsey. Haslam, meanwhile, was perfectly placed to power on to a win ahead
of Dunlop whose machine had suffered
collapsed suspension and a low-revving
engine. The Senior was won by
Irishman Norman Brown on board a
Suzuki whilst the Classic victory was
taken by Denis Ireland in a race that saw
many of the top competitors sidelined
with mechanical difficulties. Once again
it was Tony Rutter who seemed unbeat-
able in the Formula 2 on the Ducati.

For the 1983 Formula 1, Dunlop was
mounted on the new V4 Honda RS850R.

Joey's performance was astounding as he set out, Stanley Woods-style, and broke the lap record from a standing start going on to win the race at a record average speed of 114.03 mph from Grant who had used not only the entire road but the pavement as well in trying to match the Irishman's pace. The Senior Classic, the two classes having been combined, was won by Humberside's Rob McElnea on a factory Suzuki after a race-long tussle with Brown and Dunlop. Brown's race was cut short as he ran out of fuel on the third lap whilst Dunlop struggled with his Honda throughout, its handling severely altered by the increased fuel loading.

McElnea, Grant and Dunlop came head to head again at the 1984 TT. In a repeat of his 1983 success, Joey took the Formula 1 after Grant and McElnea both suffered mechanical difficulties with their factory Suzuki machines but Dunlop's win had not been without incident; on lap three he had pulled to the side of the road in a thick cloud of smoke to discover that his exhaust was rubbing against the tyre. McElnea redressed the balance in the Classic, outfoxing the Irishman using his own strategy of a single pit stop. The decider

was the Senior. Dunlop tore round the island, setting a new fastest lap on each of his first five laps, the fastest of which was at a staggering 118.47 mph. Then, with just ten ten miles remaining (about five minutes of racing), he coasted to a halt with his fuel tank empty allowing McElnea to take victory by three minutes from the Honda of Roger Marshall.

There was drama at the 1985 TT before the racing had even started. Joey Dunlop was travelling to the island aboard the fishing boat Tornamona, just as he had done since his first year of racing, when it started taking on water. RNLI lifeboats were launched as was the Air Sea Rescue Sea King. As the trawler started to sink the passengers and crew were forced to abandon ship and take to life-rafts in the dark open waters to await rescue from the stormy seas. No lives were lost but five machines belong-

BELOW Steve Hislop, 11 times winner of the TT

ing to Dunlop and Brian Reid ended up at the bottom of the Lough.

Fortunately, as Joey's works machines were already on the island it was soon business as usual as three classes fell to the Irishman at the TT. The first of these, the Formula 1 saw Joey demolish his opposition with a stunning ride that brought him to victory over five minutes ahead of Tony Rutter and Steve Parrish. Next was the Junior, a title that had eluded the Honda factory since 1967. Riding a totally unfamiliar machine he made light work of the opposition once more to win by 15 seconds from team mate Steve Cull. With the capacity limit increased to 1000cc to accommodate Formula 1 machines, Joey made his hat trick in the Senior by winning the class by 16 seconds from team mate Roger Marshall.

As the 1986 TT was hit with delays and postponements due to appalling weather conditions, Dunlop repeated his success in the Formula 1 but victory in the Senior went to Rothmans Honda team mate Roger Burnett. In an incident-packed race, Roger Marshall led from the start until a storming Trevor Nation took control on the third lap before running out of fuel. Marshall

LEFT A telephone box is covered with protective material in readiness for the TT

regained his lead but was forced to stop with a chain problem as was Dunlop when his steering damper caused problems allowing Burnett to take the lead and the win.

For 1987 Marshall had switched to the ever improving Suzuki team with Phil Mellor. Mellor led during the earlier stages of the Formula 1 until a fast-moving Dunlop showed his pace and took an advantage of 21 seconds by the time he had passed the Grandstand. Mellor responded with a class lap record but Dunlop immediately bettered him with a blistering 117.55 mph lap before heading on to take victory with a margin of fifty-two seconds. Dunlop's average race speed was faster than his fastest lap of 1986.

The Senior, postponed to the Saturday and contested over a shortened distance of four laps due to poor weather conditions, saw Loctite Yamaha's Trevor Nation take an early lead only for Dunlop to have resumed control by the end of the first lap. But then came the rain and, with Dunlop slowing, Mellor moved his way up through the field to sit just ten seconds behind the Irishman. As Joey swept out of the pits after refuelling he was soon level with Mellor on the road, although the Skoal Bandit Suzuki rider was ahead on time. Joey gradually started pulling away and with Mellor still due to pit with one lap remaining a close finish seemed guaranteed but the battle royal was not to be. Mellor, pushing a little too hard in the wet conditions, lost control of his machine negotiating The

Nook, just before Governor's Bridge, handing victory to Dunlop.

Joey's form continued through to the following year. After an inauspicious start in the production classes, the Honda rider asserted his status by taking victories in the Junior, Formula 1 and the Senior, the latter of which saw a young Steve Hislop take a creditable second place having won the Formula 2 race earlier in the week.

With Joey Dunlop sidelined through injuries sustained at Brands Hatch, the 1989 TT offered the best opportunity in many years for new talent to be seen on the top step of the Douglas podium. In the four-lap Supersport 600, Honda rider Hislop led at the end of the first lap and was never troubled on his way to victory over Dave Leach. Hislop was back on song for the Formula 1 where, despite suffering from fading brakes (or perhaps because of them!), he took a convincing win and a new absolute lap record of 121.34 mph – the first lap of the TT circuit in excess of 120 mph ever. To cap a successful week, a third win was forthcoming in the Senior where the Scotsman once again lapped at over 120 mph. Another landmark in TT history had been reached.

Chapter 10

King of the Road

IF 1989 WAS STEVE HISLOP'S YEAR to make his mark on TT history then 1990 was that of his Honda Britain team mate Carl Fogarty. 'Foggy' spent the week 'in the zone' – not communicating at all with Hislop despite sharing a garage with him. Carl later explained that the only way he knew he could beat Steve was to hate him. The two fought hard in the Formula 1 but Hislop's chances were scuppered after he was forced to pit stop with a warped front disk having overshot the course twice in one lap. After a lengthy wheel change, the Scot rejoined the race in thirty-ninth place. With just four laps remaining and the bit between his teeth he clawed his way back to ninth place, breaking the absolute lap record in the process at 122.63 mph. Fogarty, meanwhile, had finished in first place to take his first win of the week.

The Senior was run in appalling conditions has heavy rain fell on some parts of the course whilst others remained bone dry. For some riders it was too dangerous to continue and Hislop, Burnett, Dunlop and many others retired as the weather deteriorated further. But for Carl Fogarty and Phil McCallen the race was on. The two battled head-to-head until the unlucky McCallen pushed too hard and crashed, leaving Foggy to take his second win of the week.

ABOVE The tight
nature of the TT circuit
is never in doubt

OPPOSITE Carl Fogarty
in his Honda Castrol
Team leathers

The lead up to the 1991 Formula 1 was just as tense an affair as the race itself. With Honda determined to win their tenth consecutive title, both Hislop and Foggy were issued with a new HRC-prepared 145bhp RVF750R.

Both riders were determined to win and in practice offered no quarter to the other as, in turn, they recorded faster and faster laps culminating in Hislop circling the island at an amazing 124.36 mph. Youichi Oguma, the chief of HRC,

was not impressed as all he could see was an accident waiting to happen. Both riders were called to book and told in no uncertain terms to calm things down but neither was in the mood to yield to the other. For the race Hislop had a simple plan - go like stink from the off in the hope of demoralising Fogarty as soon as possible. It worked. By the time Hislop had reached the thirteenth Milestone he was already five seconds up and at Ballaugh Bridge on the second lap Foggy had been caught on the road and was thirty seconds in deficit. For the remaining laps the two duked it out together providing a great spectacle for the crowds but, for Fogarty, the damage was already done. Steve Hislop took the victory at a record average speed of 121.00 mph.

Hislop lead home a Honda one-two-three in the Senior with Joey Dunlop and Phil McCallen – Fogarty having returned to the mainland to prepare for World Superbike commitments.

Joey Dunlop was back to his winning ways again at the 1992 TT, taking the Lightweight aboard a two-stroke Honda with a record time and fastest lap. 'Hizzy' was also on form but not aboard the customary Honda that had served him so well in previous years. Hollow promises had effectively left the Scotsman without a ride for the season when he was snapped up for the TT by Barry Symmons, manager of the JPS Norton team. The Norton was a curious bike – a 588cc Rotary-engined machine developed from a police bike in the back of a shed – but it was fast. One again the race was a game of cat and mouse between Hislop and Yamaha OW01-mounted Fogarty who was taking a break from his privateer World Superbike campaign. Hislop led at the end of the fourth lap by a handful of seconds but was set back by a poor pit stop that allowed Fogarty to take advantage and the lead. By the time they had reached Ramsey, Hizzy had retaken the initiative. Despite Foggy recording a new absolute lap record at 123.61 mph on the final lap there was nothing he could do to re-catch the charging Hislop who crossed the finish line to take victory by 4.4 seconds.

Phil McCallen finally got his chance to shine at the 1993 TT by taking victory in the Senior to lead home a clean sweep of the first four placings for

Honda after losing out to Nick Jeffries in the prestigious Formula 1. Joey Dunlop maintained expectations by winning the Ultra-Lightweight with another record time and in doing so passed Mike Hailwood's all-time record of fourteen TT wins that he had equalled the previous year.

Hislop was back on song in 1994,

ABOVE Phillip MCallen in action in 1997

OPPOSITE Riders round Braddan Bridge

taking victories in both the Formula 1 and the Senior despite the best efforts of Castrol Honda team mates McCallen and Dunlop who filled the other places in the top three. Dunlop, meanwhile, added to his tally of TT wins by claiming the Ultra-Lightweight and the Junior. He had come close to not riding after his brother, Robert, had been injured in the Formula 1 but encouraging words from a hospital bed put his mind at rest.

Phil McCallen retained his Formula 1 TT title in 1995 taking the verdict by just eighteen seconds from Castrol Honda team mate Dunlop. The scales tipped firmly in the Ulsterman's favour for the Lightweight and Senior although his hope of a fourth successive Ultra-Lightweight victory was dashed as he was forced to retire after only six miles with mechanical difficulties.

Ballymena's Phil McCallen was unstoppable in his quest for glory at the 1996 TT, winning the Junior 600cc, Production classes, Formula 1 and Senior to become the only rider ever to win four TT races in a single week. His tally may well have been five but for a loss of power due to a damaged exhaust in the Lightweight that handed victory

to 'Yer Maun', Joey Dunlop. The Ultra-Lightweight was, once again, an opportunity for Joey to showcase his road craft. In a race cut short to a two-lap sprint after a delay due to poor weather, he was forced to fight his way through traffic during his first lap before drawing level with fellow Honda rider Gavin Lee with just thirteen miles to go. Blasting across a mist-soaked Mountain, Dunlop finished with a narrow 3.8 second margin over Lee to take his twenty-first career TT win.

Phil McCallen carried his success through to the 1997 TT where, despite a horrific crash at Quarry Bends during the Lightweight which was subsequently won yet again by Dunlop, he took three further

titles: the Formula 1, Production and Senior.

The 1998 TT is remembered for some of the worst racing conditions the island has ever witnessed. O'Kane Honda-rider Robert Dunlop scored an astounding win in the Ultra-Lightweight over Ian Lougher despite riding with a broken leg using a machine equipped with a left-hand front brake. His brother Joey was also nursing multiple injuries sustained at the Tandragee 100 Road Race just a few weeks before. Whereas he may not have been 100% race fit, he still had the

progressively got worse and the race was cut to just two laps his gamble paid off. With time on his side it only remained necessary for him to stay upright to secure his twenty-third TT win. Victory in the Formula 1 and Senior went to Ian Simpson in two closely contested races; his Formula 1 win was by just 2.2 seconds from Honda Britain team mate Michael Rutter whilst in the Senior he distanced Kawasaki's Bob Jackson by a mere 3.7 seconds.

A new face topped the rostrum in 1999: that of six foot two Dave Jefferies. Riding a V&M Yamaha R1, he first eclipsed Joey Dunlop in the Formula 1 before taking victory in the Production ahead of Jason Griffiths and Phil McCallen. DJ then topped his week by completely dominating the Senior despite the best efforts of his team mate Ian Duffus and Ian Lougher to unseat him. Lougher had, however, taken victory earlier that week in the Ultra-Lightweight with the Lightweight title going to John McGuinness on the Vimto Honda.

advantage of a wise and wily head on his shoulders. Riding in a Lightweight that had already been cut to three laps because of poor weather, Dunlop chose not to pit at the end of the first lap as his rivals did but to continue riding in the atrocious conditions. As the rain

As the century drew to a close, the TT's troubles looked to be in the past but, as is so often the case, fate still had a few cards to play.

Chapter 11

A New Millennium

THE FIRST TOURIST TROPHY OF the new millennium produced a fairy-tale result for Joey Dunlop, now 48 years old and at his twenty-fourth TT.

After an appalling 1999, Joey returned to the Isle of Man fully fit and with renewed vigour. Riding a specially prepared v-twin Honda SP-1, Joey stormed his way into the lead by the end of the first lap on slippery but drying roads. Only 1999 winner Dave Jefferies could match the Ulsterman's pace as he scorched his way across the Mountain but luck was not on DJ's side as on the fifth lap the clutch on his usually reliable V&M Yamaha disintegrated. Dunlop crossed the line a fraction of a second under a minute ahead of Jefferies' team mate Michael Rutter. It was an emotional and popular victory for all concerned and Dunlop's first Formula 1 triumph since 1988.

With Champagne still drying from his racing leathers, Dunlop added to his tally for the week with victories in the Ultra-Lightweight and Lightweight, his twenty-fifth and twenty-sixth TT wins respectively.

ABOVE Thousands of fans attend the funeral of Joey Dunlop

Dave Jefferies did manage to find compensation for his misfortune in the Formula 1. With the Production cut short to two laps due to heavy rain and standing water on the circuit, DJ finished almost a minute ahead of Richard Quayle although the conditions meant that times were down by over 20 mph from the previous year. To this he added the Junior aboard a V&M Yamaha R6 and the prestigious Senior ahead of Rutter and Dunlop.

Sadly the 2000 Senior was to be Joey Dunlop's last TT as just a few short weeks after leaving the Isle of Man, he lost his life whilst racing in a 125cc event in Estonia. The greatest motorcycle race in the world had lost its greatest ever son. With a tally of one hundred TT starts and twenty-six wins over a period of twenty-four years, it is unlikely the sport of motorcycle racing will ever see his like again.

With the 2001 TT cancelled due to a nationwide outbreak of Foot and Mouth disease, racing returned to the Isle of Man in the spring of 2002. Dave Jefferies picked up where he had left off two years earlier by first taking victory in the Formula 1 aboard the TAS GSX-R1000

in the Senior where he pushed the boundaries even further to record an average race speed of 124.74 mph and a new absolute lap record at 127.49 mph. For the third year the amiable Yorkshireman had achieved a hat trick of victories.

With Ian Lougher taking the Ultra-Lightweight at 108.65 mph and New Zealander Bruce Anstey recording a fastest lap of 118.03 mph in the Lightweight, 2002 was truly a year for record breaking on the Isle of Man.

There was a great deal of speculation leading up to the 2003 TT as to what Big Dave Jefferies would achieve this year. Although he had started his first TT back in 1996, the last three TTs had seen him collect a total of nine wins. Was DJ set to fill the void left by Joey Dunlop? Unfortunately the press and public did not need to wait for the start of the racing to find out.

"It is with regret that the organisers of the Isle of Man TT Races, the Auto-Cycle Union, announce that David Jefferies, of Baildon in West Yorkshire, who crashed on the second lap of this afternoon's practice session, received injuries, which proved fatal."

Once more the TT had been rocked

for which his average speed of 123.38 mph for the entire six-lap race was higher than the previous lap record for the class. This result was followed by another win in the Production 1000cc where yet more records were broken. Jefferies' final triumph of the week was

to its core and it was with a heavy heart that the racing continued. It was perhaps fitting that the 2003 Formula 1 and Senior were won by Jefferies' TAS Suzuki team mate Adrian Archibald who saw off strong challenges from the Ducati 998RS of John McGuinness and the Honda SP-1 of Ian Lougher. Anstey added to his 2002 Lightweight victory by taking the Junior to give Triumph their first TT win since 1975.

Having moved from Ducati to Yamaha, McGuinness proved he was no flash in the pan at the 2004 TT. Leading from start to finish, the rider from Morecambe set a new absolute lap record of 127.68 mph on his way to winning the opening Formula 1 race ahead of Archibald on the TAS Suzuki. Showing his versatility he then went on to take the Lightweight 400 and the Junior with new lap records in each. With his sights on a fourth win, McGuinness set a thundering pace in the Senior to lead Archibald by 21.3 seconds at the end of the second lap but his luck could not hold out. Forced to retire with clutch problems it was left to Archibald to cross the finish line in first place to take his second consecutive Senior title.

With the number of classes becoming unwieldy and outdated, the TT underwent an overhaul for 2005 with three basic categories being defined – Superbike, Supersport and Superstock – with specifications within each governing capacity.

BELOW John McGuiness on his HM Plant Honda Fireblade

A NEW MILLENNIUM

The inaugural Superbike race was another chance for McGuinness to shine as he overcame poor conditions to take the win from Archibald as retribution for the previous year's Senior. Archibald faired little better in the Superstock where, having lead from the start and with an advantage of eighteen seconds, he ran out of fuel at The Bungalow with only six miles to go to gift the title to Anstey. Lougher overcame his 2004 bad luck to win the Supersport race but was consigned to second place as once again McGuinness reigned supreme in the Senior to take victory by thirty-five seconds.

McGuinness well and truly secured his place in TT history in 2006 as he set the Manx roads alight with a series of superb performances. In the opening Superbike race he twice broke the lap record on his way to securing a 124.764 mph thirty-nine second victory over Lougher. To this he added the Supersport title, taking victory over Anstey after second-placed Ian Hutchinson was disqualified after it was found his machine breached technical regulations. The crowning glory of his week was a wonderful triumph in the Senior. Riding an HM Plant Honda Fireblade and never once troubled on his quest for victory, he broke the absolute lap record twice more taking it to an astounding 129.45 mph. McGuinness's own words sum up his performance perfectly – "It's been awesome!"

And those words perhaps define the whole experience that is the Isle of Man Tourist Trophy. The fact that the races have survived one hundred years is testament to the efforts of the organisers, the riders, the fans and the Manx population. The course may remain the same but the event has never been afraid to embrace innovation and change. It is this spirit that keeps the TT alive.

Here's to the next hundred years!

The pictures in this book were provided courtesy of the following:

GETTY IMAGES
101 Bayham Street, London NW1 0AG

CORBIS
111 Salusbury Road, London NW6 6RG

EMPICS
www.empics.com

FoTTofinders
www.amulree.com

DEPARTMENT OF TOURISM AND LEISURE
Isle of Man, IM1 2PX

Book design and artwork by Newleaf Design

Published by Green Umbrella

Publishers Jules Gammond & Vanessa Gardner

Written by Jon Stroud